Creating with
TISSUE PAPER

Creating with

TISSUE PAPER

DESIGN · TECHNIQUE · DECORATION

by

Barbara B. Stephan

CROWN PUBLISHERS, INC.
NEW YORK

Inquiries should
be addressed to Crown Publishers, Inc.,
201 East 50th Street, New York, New York 10022.

Printed in the United States of America

Library of Congress Catalog Card Number:
73-82486
ISBN 0-517-50579-7 (cloth)
ISBN 0-517-54626-4 (paper)

15   14   13   12   11

CONTENTS

Acknowledgments

It is with gratitude and appreciation that I acknowledge the generous help of those who assisted in the preparation of this manuscript. Special thanks are due my teacher in Japan, Kunio Ekiguchi, who inspired an interest in paper as an artistic medium. His students Yasuko Tomiyama, Minami Hosokawa, and above all Yumiko Tsukuda all provided unstinting aid and are responsible for a number of the designs presented here.

I would like to acknowledge the cooperation of the numerous Honolulu artists whose works are reproduced in Chapter 7. Thanks also to the British Museum, Clarendon Press, Gibson Greeting Cards, and UNICEF for permission to use illustrations of works in their possession.

The Seal Corporation of Derby, Connecticut, and Nick Wynkoop of General Binding Sales Corporation provided invaluable technical assistance relating to dry mounting and laminating. Fire Prevention Chief Andrew Yim of the Honolulu Fire Department was most helpful in recommending fireproofing methods and materials.

Heartfelt thanks are due my husband, John Stephan, for his constant cooperation and encouragement.

B.B.S.

1

INTRODUCTION

Paper as a
Decorative Material

Throughout history paper has played an important role as an aid to communication. The earliest paper, invented in China around A.D. 105 and presented to the court of Emperor Ho Ti by the eunuch Ts'ai Lun, was heralded as a welcome substitute for the costly silks on which messages, religious texts, and other writings had formerly been recorded. Though the process of papermaking was kept a secret by the Chinese for over six hundred years, the use of the material spread to the farthest reaches of the Empire, providing effective links between the authority of the central government and outlying settlements many hundreds of miles distant.

Although the Chinese originally conceived of paper in terms of writing and communication, it was not long before the decorative potential of the material they had invented was perceived. Researches in western China, where samples of paper dating back to the third and fourth century A.D. have been unearthed, have yielded such items as paper flowers, shrine ornaments, and cut paper stencils. Not only do these examples reveal a familiarity with

1

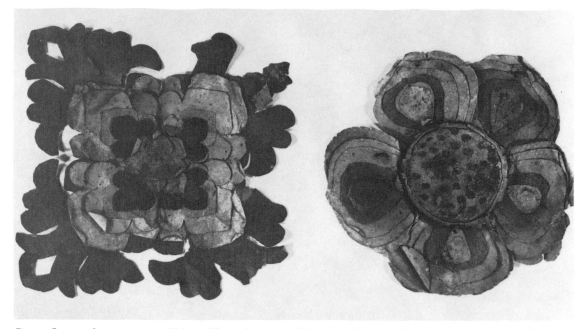

Paper flowers from western China. The colors are still vivid although the flowers are over a thousand years old. *Photograph courtesy British Museum*

such decorative techniques as cutting and folding, they also demonstrate a mastery of coloring. Even today the colors of paper flowers now in the collection of the British Museum appear nearly as vivid as when they were made over a thousand years ago.

The Chinese were unable to maintain their monopoly on papermaking beyond the eighth century, and as the technique spread both east and west, so too spread the concept of paper as a decorative material. In Japan paper was used for children's dolls, toys of papier-mâché, and as decoration on windows and doors; it also gave rise to the elaborate art of paper folding known as origami. In Europe such items as wallpaper, playing cards, and cut paper pictures came into vogue, and the technique of marbling, introduced from Persia, spurred a new interest in ways to color and decorate paper. The development of machine-made paper in the early nineteenth century and the concomitant lowering of price brought about a "boom" in the use of the material; soon paper dolls,

paper toys, and sets for the enormously popular miniature paper theatre were on sale everywhere for as little as "a penny plain, twopence coloured." So common did the material become that it was celebrated in a song entitled "The Age of Paper," popular in London music halls in the 1860s. From this period, too, come some of the early references to colored tissue paper: F. Helbronner, in a manual for Victorian ladies published in 1858, commends the use of "French Tissue Papers in all shades" for the making of paper flowers to "embellish the drawing room, the dining table, the dress."

Tissue Paper

Although over a hundred years have passed since Victorian ladies took up the craft of paper flower making, tissue paper remains one of the most popular of decorative papers produced today. The reasons for its appeal are not hard to understand.

Because of its thinness, tissue paper can be folded or stacked and cut into delicate designs. Tissue paper cutting by Yumiko Tsukuda.

First is the gossamerlike quality of the paper. Tissue paper is so thin that a number of layers can be stacked, stapled, and cut out together. Or a single sheet can be folded into sections much smaller than any thicker paper would allow, and cut to produce beautifully symmetrical designs. If a piece is pasted on a smooth surface, it rises so little above the surface that it actually appears printed, thus making tissue paper an ideal substitute for lettering on posters, for silk screening or block printing on greeting cards, or for printed or painted designs on objects such as boxes, jars, and canisters.

A second quality that makes tissue paper especially attractive is its transparency. A single sheet held to the light glows with the color of the paper; light shining through two or more overlapped sheets produces beautiful and sometimes unexpected color combinations. Because of its transparent quality, tissue paper can be used for a wide variety of projects that rely on the combined effects of color and light. Examples are lampshades, folded paper ornaments, shadow puppets, and imitation stained glass.

Next to its thinness and transparency, tissue paper is known for its striking range of colors. Depending on the manufacturer, up to forty-two colors are available; when these are combined to produce new colors the variations are almost infinite. In addition to solid colors, striped, madras, dappled, and printed varieties are available. Even white tissue paper comes in two guises: a sized variety with a surface finish like that of colored tissue, and a softer, more absorbent wrapping tissue that is particularly suitable for dyeing by hand.

In terms of brilliance the colors of tissue paper are unmatched by virtually any other paper. There is, however, a price to pay for the intensity and range of color: the colors will fade quickly in direct sunlight, and more slowly in indirect light. Some colors are much more fugitive than others: bright pink, for example, will fade perceptibly after just a few hours' exposure to the sun. Others, particularly the primary colors and black, are much more resistant. Sometimes fading is desirable: interesting prints can be made by placing opaque material such as leaves or cut paper on tissue paper and exposing it to sunlight. If necessary, however, the effects of fading can be minimized by choosing colors that are most light resistant, by covering finished work with glass or coating the surface with protective substances such as polymer medium, liquid acrylic, or lacquer, and, perhaps most important, by keeping the decorated object away from strong light.

It is also characteristic of commercial tissue paper that most of the colors run when wet. Far from being a disadvantage, this quality can be exploited creatively in a number of collage techniques. When it is important to avoid color bleeding, it is possible to work with nonwater-based ad-hesives (such as rubber cement or spray glue) or, if water-based adhesives are involved, to minimize running by spraying the paper with an aerosol plastic before glueing. Both fading and color bleeding can be controlled by hand dyeing white tissue paper following the techniques described in Chapter 7 on Collage.

A final attraction of tissue paper is its economy. At just pennies a sheet, tissue paper can be used lavishly, whether for experimentation or to cover large areas with color. Naturally, it is cheapest when purchased in large quantities: a ream (480 sheets) or a quire (24 sheets) will work out to a lower cost per 20- by 30-inch sheet than commercially marketed packages of ten or twenty sheets. The cost differential is relatively small, however, and no matter how it is purchased, tissue paper is one of the most economical art materials.

Designs in tissue paper often appear printed. These black-and-white boxes were decorated by the removal technique described in Chapter 2.

A folded ornament held to the light reveals tissue paper's transparency.

"Prints" made by exposing bright pink tissue paper to sunlight. The color of the area covered by the leaves remains unfaded.

Varieties of tissue paper include printed, striped, madras, and dappled.

HELP THE WORLD'S CHILDREN

BUY
UNICEF
CARDS

UNITED NATIONS CHILDREN'S FUND

BOX OF TWELVE CARDS—$2.00

Overlapping shapes cut from tissue paper are used to design a Christmas angel for a UNICEF poster. *Courtesy UNICEF, the United Nations Children's Fund, and Mrs. St. Tamara Kolba.*

Commercial gift-wrap paper in a charming design of torn tissue paper shapes. *Photo by permission of Buzza, a division of Gibson Greeting Cards.*

Tools

Most of the tools for working with tissue paper are those generally on hand: scissors, rulers, staplers, etc. Of the tools listed below, not all are essential, but each has a use in speeding a particular task.

Scissors. Two types are helpful: ordinary scissors for general cutting, and small curved nail scissors for detailed work.

Knives. Use a stencil knife for light work and a studio or mat knife for heavy-duty cutting. Choose styles with easily replaceable blades so that the cutting edge will

Tools for working with tissue paper. Top row (left to right): scissors, curved nail scissors, mat knife, stencil knife, swivel knife, burnisher, protractor, metal ruler. Second row: compass, stapler, two types of stylus, tweezers, nylon paintbrush. Bottom row: revolving punch, paper punch, leather punches, Japanese stencil punches, circle cutter, compass cutter.

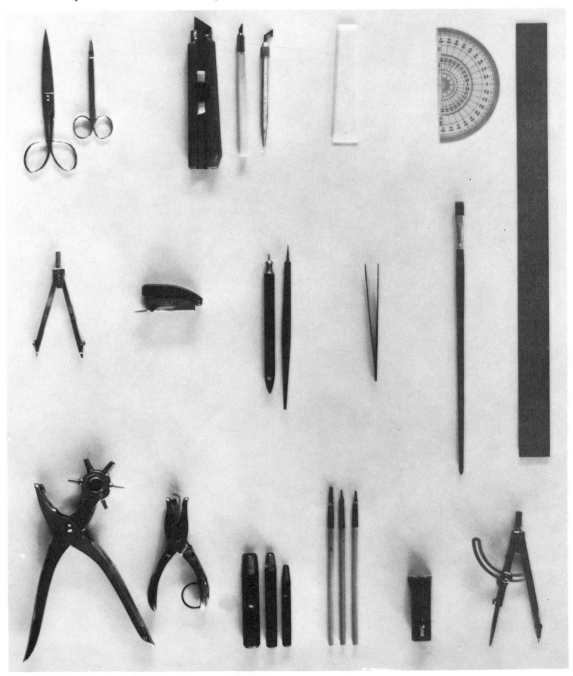

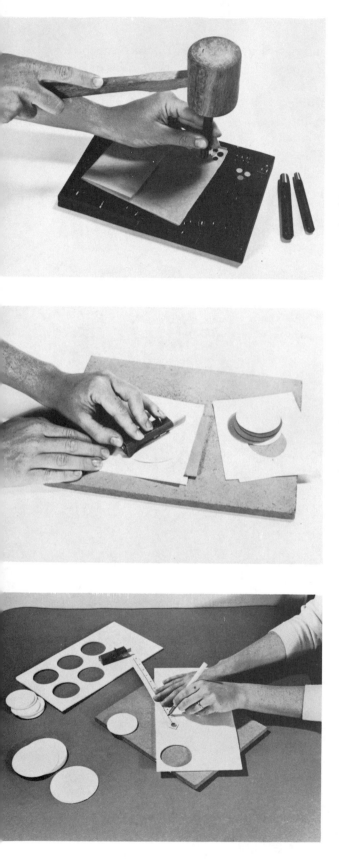

Leather punches will cut through many layers at a time. Use a rubber or wooden mallet and pounding board.

A commercial circle cutter that can cut from very small to very large circles. A piece of typing weight paper placed above and below the stack of tissue paper keeps the tissue from tearing.

A homemade circle cutter made from a strip of cardboard marked in fractions of an inch. To strengthen the cardboard strip, cover with clear adhesive-backed plastic film.

always be sharp. Avoid razor blades; they are not rigid enough to give a firm cut. A swivel knife, while not a necessity, is handy for cutting curves.

Burnisher. A flat-sided tool for burnishing tissue paper cutouts that have been glued in place with rubber cement or spray adhesive. Any similar flat-sided tool can be substituted.

Protractor. A device for measuring degrees in a circle. It is especially useful for folding paper into equal parts.

Ruler. A metal ruler or straight edge should always be used as a guide when cutting with a knife.

Compass. Essential for drawing perfect circles.

Stapler. Staples should be used liberally to hold together layers of tissue paper so that they will not slip when being cut.

Stylus. A pointed tool useful for making an indentation without leaving telltale marks. Use for tracing sketches onto paper or cardboard. A ball-point pen that has run out of ink makes a good substitute.

Tweezers. Long tweezers are especially useful for picking up small pieces of cut tissue paper.

Nylon Paintbrush. Designed for use with polymer emulsion glues and paints, nylon brushes will soak clean even if the emulsion has dried on the brush. Animal hair brushes, by contrast, require treatment in strong solvents such as acetone or lacquer thinner to remove dried glue.

Revolving Punch. Handy but not essential, a revolving punch has six different-size openings for cutting small circles from stacked tissue paper.

Paper Punch. The standard tool for cutting holes in paper.

Leather Punches. Standard sizes range from $\frac{1}{16}$ to $\frac{1}{2}$ inch, with larger sizes also available. For easy cutting they should always be used with a wooden or rubber mallet and pounding board.

Japanese Stencil Punches. Hard to obtain outside of Japan, these stencil hole-cutting tools come in infinitely small sizes.

Cardbild Circle Cutter. One of the more successful of a number of commercial circle cutters, this one comes with an extension arm for cutting circles up to 24 inches in diameter. It works very well cutting through a stack of tissue paper, provided a piece of typing weight paper is placed on top of the stack to prevent tearing.

Compass Cutter. Some compasses come equipped with a cutting blade but, because they generally lack rigidity, they are difficult to use for cutting paper.

2

TISSUE PAPER AS SURFACE DECORATION: ON PAPER AND CARDBOARD

Adhesives for use with tissue paper can generally be divided into two types: those that change the appearance of the paper, and those that do not. Water-based adhesives such as white glue and polymer medium cause tissue paper to wrinkle and the colors to bleed, qualities that can be exploited for original and interesting effects. Since special techniques are required with these glues, however, they will be considered in a separate section (see Chapter 7).

Of the adhesives that do not appreciably change the character of tissue paper, some are suited for use on paper or cardboard and some, such as lacquer or varnish, are more appropriate for use on nonabsorbent surfaces. This section deals with the techniques of applying tissue paper to paper surfaces; adhesives for use on metal, glass, and wood will be treated in the next chapter.

10

Tropical birds. Rubber cement is used as the adhesive.

Adhesives for Paper and Cardboard Surfaces

RUBBER CEMENT

When correctly applied, rubber cement provides a transparent, invisible bond between tissue paper and other paper or cardboard surfaces. Unlike water-based adhesives, it does not wrinkle the tissue paper or cause it to bleed. Whether applied directly from the container or thinned and stroked on with a brush, it dries quickly. Pieces cut from tissue paper can be repositioned before the cement dries or can be lifted after it has dried by dabbing on rubber cement thinner. Excess rubber cement, once dry, can be rubbed off easily.

Despite its suitability for use with tissue paper, rubber cement does have certain disadvantages. It is difficult to apply smoothly and can produce a splotchy effect. Because of a tendency to dry out and discolor over a period of time, it should not be used on any project considered permanent. Finally, the fumes given off by both the rubber cement and rubber cement thinner can be toxic. They should be used only in a well-ventilated room, and all precautions on the label should be strictly followed.

When working with rubber cement, start by making a sketch of the design to be used and cut out the necessary parts. If duplicate parts are needed, or if a number of copies of the same design are to be made, staple a number of layers of tissue paper together. Fasten a sheet of writing paper on top for firmness and to make cutting easier.

To transfer the design to a backing sheet —any firm paper or board will do—trace over all the lines using a stylus or other pointed instrument. This will transfer the pattern by means of light indentations on the backing board, eliminating the mess of carbon paper. Next, using your finger or a brush, spread rubber cement on one area of the design. If the consistency seems too thick, thin by mixing in rubber cement

When cutting a number of layers of tissue paper at one time, prevent slipping by stapling a sheet of paper to the pile to be cut.

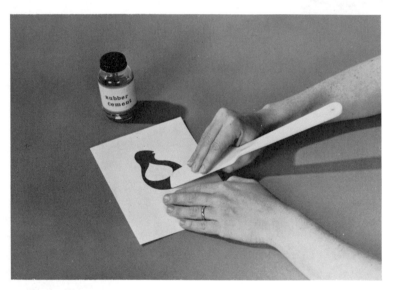

Spreading the glue carefully is the secret of a firm and neat bond. Excess glue is allowed to dry, then rubbed away.

Cut away unneeded parts with a stencil knife. Dab on a little rubber cement thinner if removal is difficult.

thinner. While the cement is still wet, slide the piece of tissue paper into place. Using a flat instrument such as a spatula or glue spreader, smooth out any wrinkles, squeezing excess rubber cement out from under the paper where it can be rubbed away when dry. Work gently to avoid tearing the fragile tissue.

Overlapping parts can be cut away with the light stroke of a stencil knife. If the tissue paper does not lift easily, dab on a little rubber cement thinner. Mistakes can be removed in the same way.

SPRAY ADHESIVE

Spray adhesive has most of the advantages of rubber cement with few of the drawbacks. It is easily applied, transparent when dry, and does not wrinkle or discolor tissue paper. Because only a thin coat is necessary, the buildup inevitable with rubber cement is avoided. Material can be repositioned before the spray dries, or can be lifted after it dries by using solvents such as rubber cement thinner or lighter fluid.

Different brands of spray adhesive come in different strengths, not always indicated by the manufacturer. It is worthwhile experimenting with several types, but generally a light or medium bond is most suitable. Sprays that emphasize their ability to bond cloth or other heavy materials should be avoided; they grip too firmly and allow no chance for repositioning.

Certain precautions are advisable when using aerosol adhesives. First, to avoid clogging the spray tip, make sure to invert the can after each use and press the tip until the spray is clear of adhesive. This is much easier than trying to clean a clogged tip in solvent. Second, always observe the manufacturer's warnings. Aerosol products are in general highly flammable and must be kept away from heat and flame. Like rubber cement, the fumes can be toxic, so care should be taken to use the spray in a well-ventilated room.

Spray adhesive is easy to work with: simply spray the back of a piece of tissue paper and smooth it into place on the backing board. If the paper is incorrectly placed, lift it with tweezers and reposition, then rub with a flat-sided tool to ensure good adhesion.

Spray adhesive is also helpful in working with delicate shapes that wrinkle or tear easily. These require special treatment: rather than spraying the tissue paper directly, coat a piece of thin cardboard with just enough adhesive to make it tacky. Use this card to pick up the tissue and hold it flat while the back of the cutout is sprayed with adhesive. The card can then be laid face down over the spot where the tissue paper is to be positioned, burnished lightly, and lifted, leaving the tissue design neatly in place.

Interesting designs can also be created using spray adhesive for a removal technique. Instead of cutting out a pattern before glueing the tissue paper, use a stencil knife to score the tissue once it has been glued. Unwanted areas can then be loosened with solvent and removed, leaving a design based on the contrast between areas of light and dark. The technique is especially suited to geometric or op art designs, but naturalistic themes can also be effective.

An improvised light box makes it possible to copy a design sketched in dark ink. Place a light bulb inside a cardboard box, cover the top with a piece of glass, and hold the sketch under the paper to which tissue paper has been glued. With the light turned on, the lines of the sketch become visible and can be followed with a stencil knife.

Delicate shapes are likely to tear unless applied carefully. Lay the pattern face up on a flat surface and coat a piece of firm paper or thin cardboard *very lightly* with spray cement.

Use a rolling motion to pick up the tissue paper design.

Coat the design with spray cement.

Lay the design in place, rub lightly, and carefully pull away the backing card. Use a flat-sided implement to smooth out any wrinkles.

When shapes cut from one piece of paper are glued to an adjacent space, a positive-negative design is created. Repeating the motifs has a decorative effect.

Boxes with a positive-negative design.

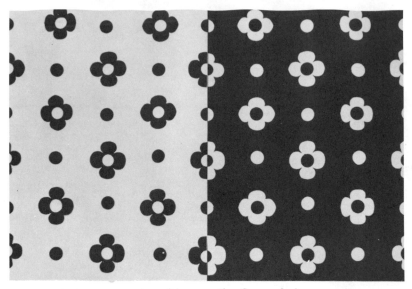

A positive-negative flower design.

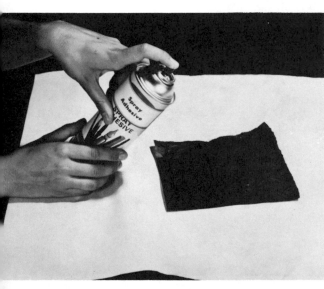

Coat tissue paper with spray adhesive.

Apply to a paper or cardboard backing and rub to remove wrinkles and ensure a good bond.

Make light cuts through the tissue paper using an ordinary stencil knife or (for curves) a swivel-blade knife. Do not cut through the backing paper.

Apply rubber cement thinner with a cotton-tipped swab to areas to be lifted. The pattern emerging here is based on cutting random curves and removing every other piece.

An exercise in black and white. Black tissue paper was glued to a white backing with spray cement, and a stencil knife used to cut away parts of the design. A light box was used to make the lines of a grid sketched on graph paper visible through the backing sheet; the grid provided the guidelines for cutting the designs shown here.

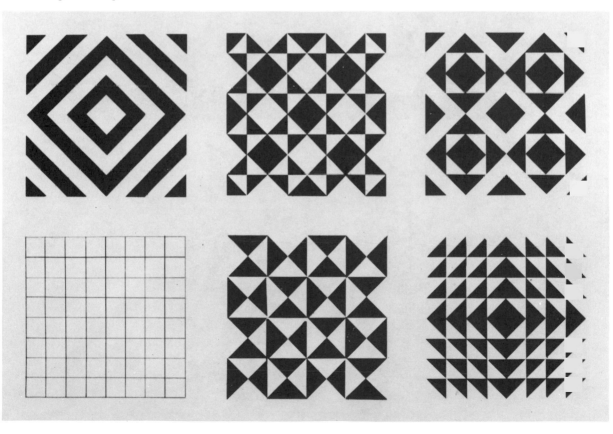

Abstract designs cut from circles. These would also make attractive coasters.

A zebra fish emerges from a pattern of waves.

ADHESIVE-BACKED FILM

Instead of using an ordinary adhesive, it is possible to secure a tissue paper design using transparent adhesive-backed plastic film. The result is much like a decal, and if an adequate margin of film is allowed, the design can be cut out and fastened to a window for a stained-glass effect or to a light-colored surface for a printed appearance. The technique is especially useful for making multiple copies of a single pattern. It is not, however, suitable for designs that have many overlapping parts, since not all the tissue would be secured by the adhesive film.

To make a decal first draw the design on a sheet of paper and cut the necessary pieces out of tissue paper. Remove the backing from a piece of transparent film and thumbtack the film in place, adhesive side up, over the drawing. Lay the appropriate parts on the film with tweezers, replace the backing sheet, and trim the decal. It is then ready for use whenever the backing sheet is removed.

Adhesive-backed film can also be used to protect surfaces that are already decorated with tissue paper designs. Place mats, boxes, playing cards, and other objects subject to constant handling will be ruined by dirt and moisture unless sealed. To cover a large surface without wrinkles requires a little care, but certain tricks can help to ensure success.

First, cut a sheet of film slightly larger all around than the surface to be covered. Wrap this around a paper towel roll or other round object with the backing on the outside. Separate a small area of adhesive film from its backing, and secure to one edge of the surface to be covered. Slowly pull away the backing sheet, rolling the tube forward, and the film should adhere smoothly. To ensure a good bond, rub the whole surface from the center outward with the side of a flat-edged tool.

It should be noted that several thicknesses of adhesive-backed plastic are available—a heavier, kitchen quality sold in variety stores, and a thinner, smooth-surfaced film found in stationery and art supply stores. The thinner film is preferable; it provides a smoother, more professional-looking finish.

Clear adhesive-backed film substitutes for glue in making tissue paper decals. Lay the film adhesive side up over the drawing and apply the cutout parts with tweezers.

Butterfly decal used on a greeting card. By Yumiko Tsukuda.

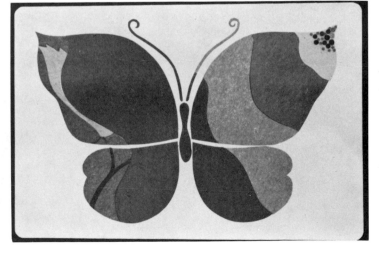

Adhesive-backed film secures these "embroidered ribbon" designs to their paper backing.

Cut a piece of film slightly larger than the area to be covered and roll around a cardboard tube with the backing on the outside.

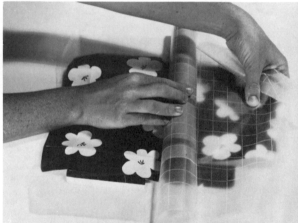

Roll on the film while pulling away the backing sheet.

Work from the center out to smooth the film in place.

Adhesive-backed film can be used both as a glue and as a protective covering. Scraps of tissue paper are scattered on the sticky side of the film and it is then wrapped around a box.

LAMINATING FILM

Adhesive-backed film offers a practical, easily applied finish for articles decorated with tissue paper designs, but it can yellow or become sticky after a number of years' use. If a more permanent finish is desired, a similar but superior product is available: Mylar laminating film.*

Made of a tough, nonyellowing plastic coated with a heat-sensitive material, laminating film can be bonded to almost any flat surface when subjected to heat and pressure. Although intended for use in a laminating press, it can be successfully applied to small surfaces with an ordinary home iron. While it is especially useful as a protective coating for decorated surfaces, it can also substitute as an adhesive for

* Laminating film can generally be obtained at photographic supply stores. For sources in your area, see the Index of Suppliers at the back of this book.

adhering delicate designs. If a cutout is too large or fragile to apply with ordinary glues, it can be tacked lightly in place with a tiny amount of rubber cement and then laminated.

To apply laminating film first cut a sheet of film larger than the item to be covered. If sealing both sides, fold the laminating film (dull side inward) to make a sandwich. Insert this between sheets of clean paper and apply an iron set at low to medium temperature (generally between rayon and wool, but the proper setting may vary with the iron). Hold the iron in one place for about ten seconds, then lift and immediately rub the heated area with a crumpled cloth or paper towel. The adhesive is melted by the heat of the iron, but bonding takes place only as the material cools, so the rubbing step is essential to ensure a complete seal. If there are any air pockets left, repeat the heating and rubbing process. For larger items treat the surface section by section. To speed the process use one hand to rub the area just heated while the other hand holds the iron over the next area to be treated.

If you have an especially large surface to cover, you may wish to leave the job to a professional. Look under "dry mounting" or "laminating" in the yellow pages of the telephone directory or consult any firm (such as a picture framer's) that uses a dry mounting press.

Delicate or lacy designs can be held in place with heat-sensitive laminating film. This cutout (for a book illustration) was sealed in a laminating press, but a hand iron can also be used to seal small surfaces. By Yumiko Tsukuda.

Cut laminating film slightly larger than the design to be covered. This playing card is to be covered on both sides, so the film is folded, dull side inward, to make a sandwich.

Cover with a sheet of paper and press with an iron set at low to medium temperature for approximately 10 seconds.

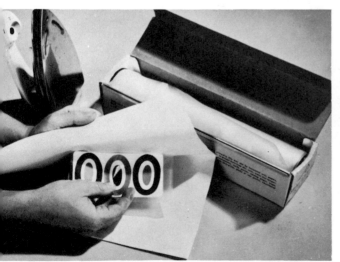

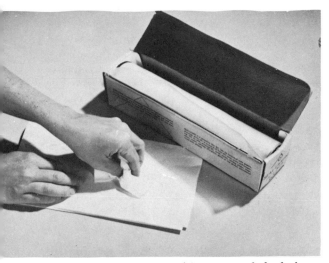

Rub the heated area with a crumpled cloth or paper towel.

Trim away the excess film. If any unsealed pockets remain, repeat the process.

A deck of hand-designed playing cards. Laminating film protects the surfaces from moisture and dirt.

DRY MOUNTING TISSUE

One other product, also intended for use in dry mounting, can be borrowed by the craftsman for use with tissue paper. This is a dry mounting tissue characterized by a white, waxy surface.* While most dry mounting tissues require the high heat of a dry mounting press, the waxy type can be applied with a warm iron. It is especially useful for attaching large pieces of tissue paper that might wrinkle if another adhesive were used. It can also be used to join two sheets of tissue to produce the two-colored paper described in Chapter 11.

To cut out a pattern in tissue and dry mounting paper, lay a piece of the dry mounting material on a piece of tissue paper and place the design on top. Go over the design with a stylus or other pointed instrument. The pressure will cause the waxy sheet to stick to the tissue paper, and both sheets can be cut out together.

Next lay this double layer on the paper or board to which it is to be attached. Score with a blunt instrument to hold both sheets in place. Cover with a sheet of clean paper, and repeat the pressing and rubbing procedure used for laminating: that is, hold the warm iron in place for about ten seconds, then immediately rub the heated area to ensure good adhesion. Should any of the waxy substance seep out from under the edges of the tissue paper, it can be wiped away with a solvent such as rubber cement thinner. Likewise, should you make a mistake, simply re-press to melt the wax and then lift off the undesired piece, cleaning the residue with solvent.

* Fotoflat, a waxy dry mounting tissue manufactured by the Seal Company of Derby, Connecticut, can be purchased at photographic supply stores.

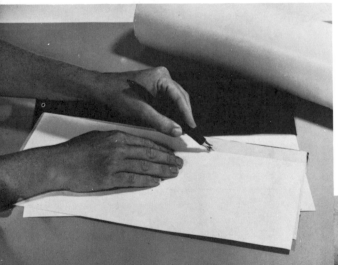

Lay the pattern pieces on a backing sheet (here illustration board is used) and mark with X's to hold in place.

Lay the dry mounting paper on a sheet of tissue and cover with the design (here a curved line cut from cardboard). Draw the design with a stylus or other pointed instrument. The dry mounting paper will adhere to the tissue, making the pattern easy to cut.

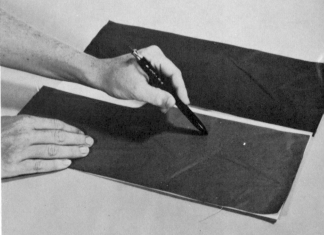

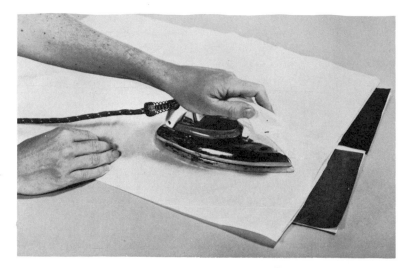

Cover with paper and press, one section at a time, with a warm iron.

Immediately after heating each section, rub with a crumpled cloth or paper towel to ensure a good bond.

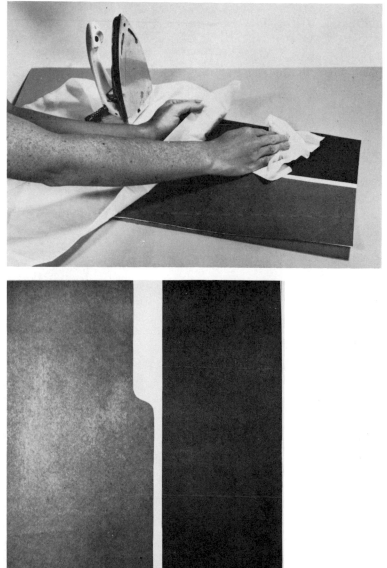

Heat-sensitive dry mounting tissue is an effective adhesive for designs with large areas of opaque color.

Projects for Paper Surfaces

POSTERS AND LETTERING

It is often impractical to print small numbers of posters, yet it may be too time-consuming to redraw them one by one. Tissue paper, being inexpensive and easy to cut, makes an ideal substitute for printing. Ten or more layers can be cut at one time, making it not much more difficult to produce ten posters than to produce one.

Lettering can be designed freehand, or stencils can be used for a uniform effect. Once the parts are cut, their placement on the poster can be juggled to find the best effect. The exercise in lettering illustrated shows the variety of effects possible just by varying the position and spacing of the letters used.

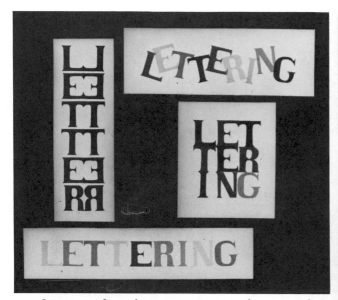

Letters cut from the same pattern can be arranged for a variety of effects.

Design for a book jacket with tissue paper lettering. The overlapping letters emphasize tissue paper's transparent quality.

GREETING CARDS

Greeting cards may be designed and made individually, or, when many are desired, duplicate pieces can be cut as an efficient means of turning out a large number of cards. Endless variations are possible: the New Year's card relies on the stark effect of dark tissue on a white background, while the dainty flower designs shown em-phasize the transparency of tissue paper by building up overlapping parts. The Merry Christmas cards are drawn in pen and ink with tissue paper dots and bows as color accents. Still another effect is achieved in the cut stencil illustration, where a black overlay (which could be either tissue or construction paper) gives the appearance of stained glass.

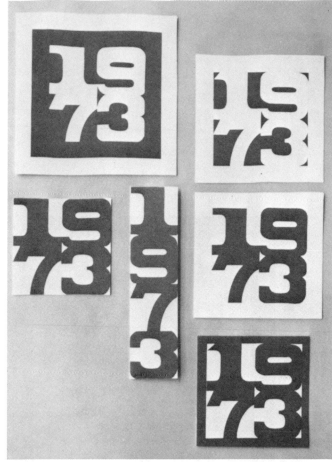

An assortment of New Year's cards based on variations of a single design. They appear printed rather than glued.

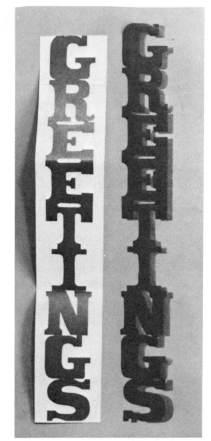

A long and narrow greeting card folds into thirds.

The letters in this card are mere empty space; they are defined only by the areas of color around them.

Overlapping shapes underline tissue paper's transparency. By Yumiko Tsukuda.

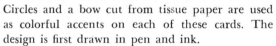

Circles and a bow cut from tissue paper are used
as colorful accents on each of these cards. The
design is first drawn in pen and ink.

Place cards made by the removal technique. Tissue paper is glued down with spray cement, the design cut with a stencil knife, and rubber cement thinner applied to loosen the areas to be removed. By Yumiko Tsukuda.

A birthday card bouquet. The lettering is done with a felt pen. By Yumiko Tsukuda.

◄

A stained glass effect produced by glueing a black paper stencil over colored tissue paper. By Yumiko Tsukuda.

CALENDARS

Three kinds of calendars are illustrated. One is a perpetual calendar designed to be fastened to a metallic surface, with magnets used to mark the date. A second type requires individual cards to be made for the seven days of the week, thirty-one days of the month, and twelve months of the year.

To protect the surfaces from fingerprints, each card is covered with clear adhesive-backed plastic. A third variation uses an animal motif for each month of the year. The days of the month are applied using instant transfer lettering (available in stationery stores), which is held over the spot to be printed and rubbed on.

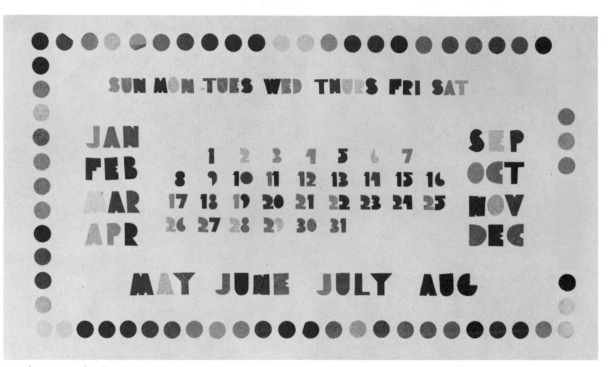

A perpetual calendar in rainbow colors. Magnets are used to mark the date, month, and day of the week.

Cards announcing the date are covered with clear adhesive-backed plastic for protection.

The animals are cut from black tissue paper and details drawn in with a felt pen. Instant transfer letters and numbers give a professional appearance.

BOXES

Whether intended as gift boxes or as an exercise in package design, boxes provide an ideal surface for decoration with tissue paper. Use a firm but flexible card such as two- or three-ply bristol board. For construction details, follow the diagrams given here, examine bakery and department store packages, or experiment with your own designs. For durability, be sure to cover the surfaces with adhesive-backed plastic or laminating film. Avoid, however, covering the flaps that are to be glued, since most glues do not adhere well to plastic-covered surfaces.

Diagram for a sealed cube. Decorate while flat, then cover all but the flaps with clear adhesive-backed film. Assemble by glueing the flaps.

Boxes are first covered with colored tissue paper, then scored with random curves and alternate sections removed.

A sophisticated play toy. Blocks with a different design on each side can be combined in a variety of patterns. These are in red, white, and blue.

Diagram for a box that opens at the top. Only the side flap requires glueing. The bottom flaps can be pushed inward to fold the box flat for storage.

Gift boxes in a flower design with matching greeting cards.

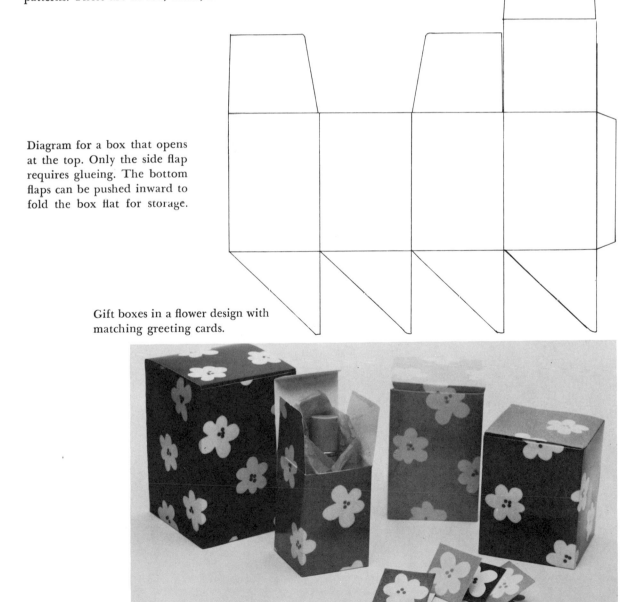

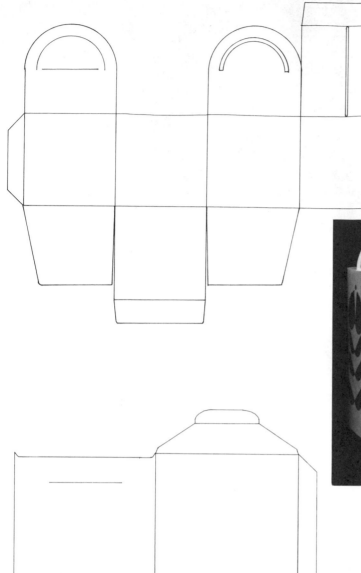

Diagram for a box with handles. Bend the handles on the two side flaps upward, and close the third flap over them.

The flowers, made entirely from circles cut in half, "grow" from the small box to the largest; the handle repeats the circular theme.

Envelope diagram.

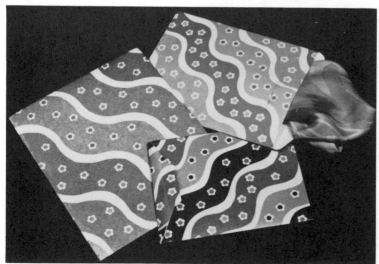

Colorful envelopes make good gift packages for flat objects.

Calico pears pose jauntily on a picnic box. By Yumiko Tsukuda.

Floral shapes are applied randomly to decorate a letter holder. By Yumiko Tsukuda.

A colorful bird perches on the cover of a letter case. Inside are pockets for writing paper and envelopes. By Yumiko Tsukuda.

PICTURES

Frame a design of tissue paper and you have a decorative accent for any room. Don't, however, count on its lasting forever, for (as explained in Chapter 1) the colors of the tissue will eventually fade in room light. You can lengthen the life of any picture by: (1) keeping it out of direct sunlight, (2) framing under glass, and (3) avoiding the most fugitive colors (see Chapter 1). In cases where permanence is a prime concern, the tissue paper should be hand-dyed, even though this may mean some sacrifice in color brilliance when compared to commercially dyed tissue.

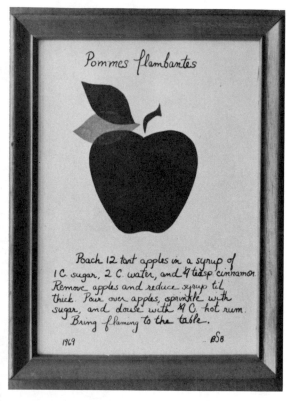

Recipe cards with tissue paper designs are complemented by bright spray-painted frames.

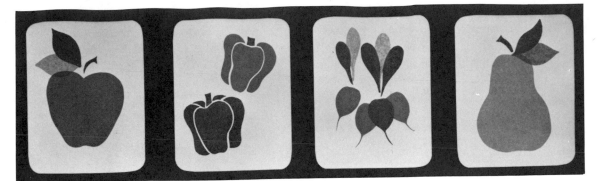

Fruits and vegetables to enliven a kitchen wall.

A whimsical monkey swings through a tissue paper jungle.

OTHER USES

The use of tissue paper as surface decoration does not have to be confined to the projects already mentioned; with imagination it can be used on almost any flat, light-colored surface. It could, for instance, be applied in a large mural directly to a plaster wall, or to the ceiling as a temporary party decoration. Playing cards are a possible use—those illustrated were made using spray cement to hold the red and black tissue designs in place, and transfer lettering was applied to label the cards. Or try a fort cut from lightweight foam core board (Styrofoam faced with paper) and covered with clear adhesive-backed plastic for perma-

nence. Foam core board can also be decorated and cut into jigsaw puzzles, puppets, circus animals, and other imaginative shapes.

Word cards can also be assembled to make a three-dimensional construction.

Cutting paper-faced Styrofoam (polystyrene foam) board. A large craft knife and a metal-edged ruler are essential.

Apply tissue paper with spray cement, then cover the surface with adhesive-backed plastic film.

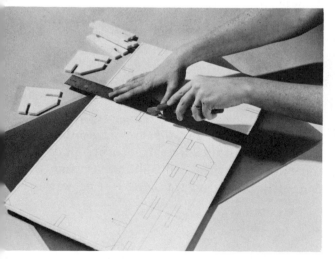

A fort from foam core board. The material is lightweight but surprisingly strong.

3

TISSUE PAPER ON METAL, GLASS, AND WOOD

Paper is not the only surface to which tissue paper can be applied. If the proper techniques are used, materials such as glass, metal, and wood can also be decorated. Naturally, such nonabsorbent surfaces call for stronger adhesives than those used with paper, especially since the articles decorated are often subject to considerable wear. Luckily, there are available a number of materials that can serve both as an adhesive and as a protective, waterproof coating.

Adhesives

Varnish and lacquer provide a strong bond between tissue paper and the smooth surfaces of glass, metal, or wood. Varnish, however, has a yellowish cast that is accentuated with age, so care should be taken to coat only the tissue paper being applied and not the surrounding area. Lacquer is crystal clear and can be used on unpainted glass and metal or on wood that has been coated with a water-based latex paint. Its strong solvent base makes it unsuitable for use over most spray-painted surfaces, however, since it tends to dissolve the underlying coating.

Liquid acrylic glaze avoids the drawbacks of both varnish and lacquer: it is nonyellow-

Orange tissue paper in an allover pattern decorates a metal chest spray-painted yellow.

These canisters looked old and worn until they were repainted and decorated with tissue paper cutouts.

A wall switch plate is exposed to both light and wear. To prevent fading, paint or dye the tissue paper; to protect the surface from fingermarks, give several light coatings with clear spray acrylic.

ing and can be used over most painted surfaces. Generally sold in small bottles as "glaze" * (available in hobby shops), it is similar in makeup to the aerosol acrylic often referred to as "spray plastic." Like lacquer and varnish, this versatile product can be used both as an adhesive and as a waterproof protective coating.

Water-based polymer emulsion glue (usually known as "white glue") also has a limited usefulness in adhering tissue paper to glass, metal, or wood. Although it causes the colors of the tissue to bleed, white glue can be used in conjunction with spray adhesives in certain circumstances.

A Note on Color

If the object to be decorated is intended for long use, hand coloring or dyeing of the tissue paper should be considered. The tissue used for the wall switch plates on page 41 was painted with acrylic emulsion paints, while the paper for the yellow metal picnic box on page 44 was dip-dyed. These coloring techniques, which guarantee greater permanence, are described in detail in Chapter 7.

Decorating Glass and Metal

The first step in decorating either glass or metal objects is to make sure the surface is spotlessly clean. Wash in hot soapy water or clean with a solvent such as turpentine or rubber cement thinner. If metal surfaces are to be painted, a light sanding with fine sandpaper will ensure better adhesion. When painting, use any light-colored spray enamel or lacquer. To avoid sagging, spray a number of very light coats rather than one or two heavy ones. Don't forget the basic precautions when using aerosol products: keep away from heat and flame, and

* See the Index of Suppliers at the back of this book.

use only in a well-ventilated area.

Once the paint has dried, the tissue paper can be applied. Squeeze a small amount of acrylic glaze into a dish, and brush this either directly on the surface to be decorated or on the tissue paper cutout. Apply the cutouts with tweezers, then brush on another light coat of glaze. (Brushes can later be cleaned in turpentine.) Before the acrylic glaze dries, the tissue paper can be freely repositioned; once dry, however, it holds firmly.

For added protection, spray the surface with several light coats of acrylic spray. This clear plastic, if sprayed into a dish or bottle cap, can also be brushed on as a substitute for the liquid acrylic glaze. It is, however, faster drying and somewhat more difficult to work with.

Prepare glass and metal surfaces by (1) washing or cleaning with a solvent, (2) lightly sanding painted surfaces to ensure that successive coats of spray paint adhere well.

To avoid overspray, place the object to be painted in a box. Give several light coats of any light-colored spray lacquer or enamel.

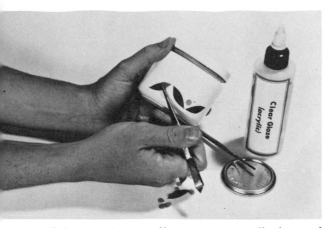

Paint on clear acrylic glaze as an adhesive, and apply cutout pieces of tissue paper with tweezers. The pieces can be repositioned as long as the glaze is wet.

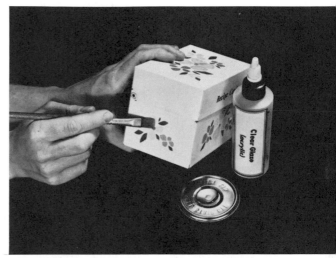

To protect the completed design, coat the surface of the tissue paper with acrylic glaze. Several coats from an aerosol can of spray acrylic could also be used.

Jam jars with fruit motifs. In this way kitchen castaways can be turned into useful objects.

Spray paint and tissue paper transform a dull gray file box into a cheery recipe holder. Recipe cards can be decorated with a matching design.

Whimsical animals pose on tea canisters. They could also be used as children's blocks.

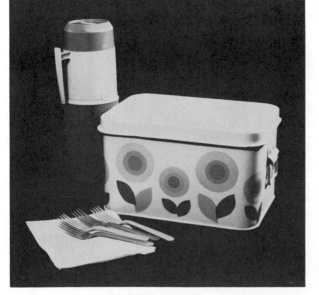

A yellow picnic box sprouts a garden of flowers. Since it will be exposed to the sun, hand-colored paper is used.

A second technique combines spray adhesive and white glue for use in circumstances that require cutting and removing tissue paper that is already applied—as, for example, in creating the circular designs decorating the candy tins on page 46.

You can minimize the tendency of the water-based white glue to cause bleeding by spraying the tissue paper first with a coat of clear spray acrylic. When this has dried, apply spray adhesive to the back of the tissue paper and attach the shape to the object to be decorated, smoothing it carefully in place. In the case of the candy tins,

bottle caps provide a cutting guide. Unwanted segments are pulled away (use rubber cement thinner if any part adheres stubbornly), leaving a design of concentric rings. These are then painted with a white glue mixture—the thinned glue has the advantage of penetrating the tissue paper to provide a firm bond with the metal below. When the glue has dried to a transparent protective coating, wipe off any excess with a sponge dipped in water. Several light coats of spray acrylic will further protect the surface.

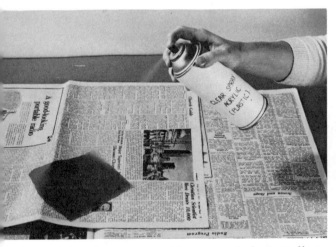

Spray tissue paper with a coat of clear acrylic to reduce the bleeding inevitable when colored tissue paper is applied with a water-based glue.

Coat the back of the tissue paper with spray cement, then smooth into place.

Using a stencil knife and light pressure, cut through the tissue paper. Lift off the extraneous pieces (use rubber cement thinner if necessary).

Paint over the tissue paper with a mixture of white glue and water. Some wrinkles will form, but they will generally disappear when the tissue paper dries. To speed drying, use a portable hair dryer.

Wipe off any smudges or excess glue with a sponge dipped in water, then spray the completed design with several light coats of spray acrylic.

Painted and decorated candy tins can be used to hold knickknacks.

Round trays also make use of the spray cement and white glue method.

Metal box with a striking overall design. Since black tissue paper does not run when wet, it can be applied using white glue.

A punch was used to cut out circles from folded black tissue paper, and the pieces applied using spray cement and white glue.

Decorating Wood

Wood surfaces can be treated exactly like metal and glass; that is, they can be spray painted and then decorated using clear acrylic glaze or white glue. But there is also another alternative. Latex house paint, which adheres readily to wood but is not a successful covering for glass or metal, can be brushed on as a base coat, and lacquer used as the adhesive for applying the tissue paper. Since the latex paint is a water-based emulsion, it is not attacked by the solvent-based lacquer as spray enamels are.

The procedure is as follows. First prepare the wood by sanding to a smooth, even finish. Cracks or blemishes can be filled with spackle or wood putty. Once the surface is prepared, brush on latex paint, using two coats if necessary. The paint should be of the proper brushing consistency directly from the can, but it can be thinned with water if desired. (Brushes should also be cleaned with water.) When the surface is dry, apply tissue paper designs using clear brushing lacquer as both adhesive and protective coating. Pieces can be readjusted while the lacquer is wet, but care should be taken in placing the tissue paper cutouts, as the lacquer dries rather quickly. The brushes used for applying lacquer can be cleaned in lacquer thinner, a strong solvent that should be handled with care.

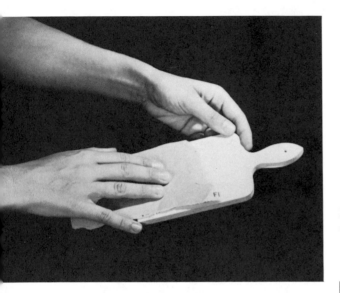

Before painting wood, sand the surface and fill any cracks with Spackle or wood putty.

Brush on latex house paint, a water-based emulsion that is not dissolved by lacquer.

Apply tissue paper cutouts using clear brushing lacquer.

A small breadboard becomes a note pad to hang in the kitchen.

(Below) Amusing designs cut from tissue paper and applied with clear lacquer decorate these wooden blocks for children.

Transfer Lettering

With a little care, instant transfer lettering can be applied to surfaces of metal, glass, or wood, providing a professional-looking finish. If the lettering is to be used on a painted surface, it helps to sand the surface lightly to ensure adhesion. Place the transfer lettering sheet over the area to be lettered, and rub with a pencil or other instrument until the letter separates from its backing and attaches itself to the painted surface. Bolder scripts are more successful than delicate ones; lacy letters tend to shatter on being applied to a hard surface. Finish by spraying with several coats of clear acrylic to protect the lettering from handling and cleaning.

Sanding a painted surface improves adhesion when transfer lettering is rubbed on. To protect the lettered surface, coat with a clear acrylic spray.

Transfer lettering labels these spice cans, each decorated with a different color flower.

4

DECORATED EGGS

Decorating the curved surface of an egg-shell can be a trying task. Paintbrushes are unsteady, felt pens generally blur, and steel pens tend to spatter. Tissue paper solves most of these problems. Cutting gives a clean, crisp line hard to imitate with brush or pen. The tissue is so thin that over a dozen duplicate pieces can be cut at one time. When these thin pieces are applied to an eggshell, the designs appear to be printed rather than glued to the surface.

Water-based emulsions (such as white glue or polymer medium) or clear glazes of the acrylic or lacquer type are the best adhesives for applying tissue paper to an eggshell. As well as holding the design in place and protecting against dirt and moisture, they also help to strengthen the egg's otherwise fragile surface.

Preparing the Egg

The first step is to empty the egg. A strong needle or an ice pick are both suitable tools for making holes in an egg, but a pointed knife does the neatest job. Hold the egg firmly in one hand, and with the other hand slowly press the knife point into one end of the egg. As soon as the shell is penetrated,

A crane cut from black tissue paper is applied with thinned white glue.

A sassy bear with upturned nose personalizes this egg.

begin rotating the knife blade, using only light pressure, until a perfectly round hole is made. Repeat at the other end of the egg, and then blow out the contents into a bowl. The blowing will be much easier if a toothpick or skewer is inserted into the egg to break the yolk and ease any clogging.

Rinse the shells by blowing a mouthful of water through them, and then stand on a rack to dry. Drying can be hastened by placing the rack in a warm (200°F.) oven for ten to fifteen minutes, after which the shells are ready for use.

If the process of emptying eggs seems tedious, there is the alternative of hard-boiling the eggs. As long as a hard-boiled egg has no cracks its contents will not spoil, but will eventually turn to powder through dehydration. Hollow eggs, however, have certain advantages: they are lighter, easier to store, and can be adapted for mobiles and other hanging decorations.

To empty an eggshell, carefully open a hole in either end. Break the yolk using a long needle or skewer, and blow out the contents.

Planning a Design

In planning a design for an eggshell, there are several simple points to remember. The first is obvious—eggs have a curved surface. Thus, a design planned on flat paper may not work out when applied to the egg. If it is necessary to sketch a design beforehand, hold a small piece of white tissue paper over the egg, draw the desired shape on the tissue, and then use this pattern to cut the finished pieces from black or colored tissue. This technique can also be used to create a design whose parts fit together almost like a puzzle. First a piece of black tissue of random shape is cut and glued, then a second shape is traced on white tissue to fit next to the first. One by one additional pieces are sketched, cut, and glued, until the surface of the egg is covered.

The egg's curved surface is not the only feature that can be troublesome. It is also helpful to remember a second point—all eggs differ from one another in size and shape. For some designs this variation is of little importance, but for any pattern that completely encircles the egg each piece of tissue must be measured individually. Do this by wrapping a strip of tissue once around the length or breadth of an egg and trimming off any overlap. This strip can then be folded and cut into a design that will fit the shell perfectly.

To cut a design whose parts fit together while still accommodating the curved surface of the eggshell, first sketch the pattern on a piece of white tissue paper held against the egg.

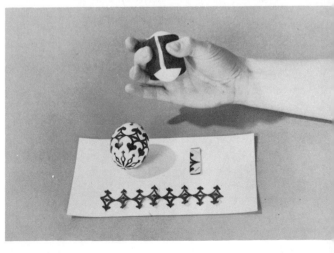

Designs that encircle the egg should be measured to ensure perfect fit. Trim a strip of tissue paper to size, then fold and cut it in the desired pattern.

Assorted designs using black tissue paper. The all-black egg was covered with strips of tissue from which a design had been cut.

Emulsion Glues and
Black Tissue Paper

Black tissue paper, which does not run when wet, can be applied using either thinned white glue or polymer medium (a material used in painting with polymer paints). Both are emulsions of plastic resin in water. Milky white when applied, they dry to a transparent, waterproof film. Water can be used both to thin the emulsions and to wash out the brushes after use.

To apply, use an ordinary brush or one with nylon bristles designed for use with polymer paints. Thin the glue to brushing consistency with water, then coat one segment of the egg. Press on the tissue cutout, using either fingers or a paintbrush to flatten any creases. The design can be shifted as long as the glue remains wet. Once a piece is correctly positioned, paint over the design once more with the glue and water mixture.

Black tissue paper designs can be applied with a water-based adhesive such as white glue or polymer medium. Coat the egg's surface, press on the tissue paper, then cover with a second coat of adhesive. Rinse brushes in water after each use.

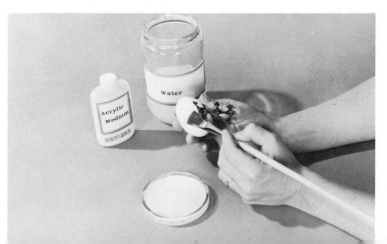

Colored Tissue Paper

Colored tissue paper can be applied using either clear lacquer or acrylic glaze (sold in hobby shops) as the adhesive. The procedure is the same as with the emulsion glues: coat an area of the eggshell with glaze, apply the tissue paper designs, then brush on an overcoat of glaze. Should it be necessary to remove a piece that has dried in place, apply lacquer thinner (the solvent for lacquer) or turpentine (the solvent for acrylic glaze) and lift off the loosened tissue paper. These same solvents should also be used for cleaning brushes.

Whether using a water- or solvent-based glue, work on only half the eggshell at a time, then allow the adhesive to dry before completing the design. Once finished, paint the whole egg with a final coat of glue or glaze (whichever you have been using) and prop it on the end of a skewer stuck in clay or Styrofoam to dry. This final coating protects the tissue, strengthens the shell of the egg, and adds a beautiful glossy finish.

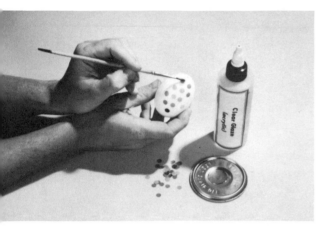

Colored tissue paper would run if applied with a water-based adhesive; instead use lacquer or clear acrylic glaze.

Designs cut from colored tissue paper are held in place with liquid acrylic glaze. An extra coat of glaze strengthens the hollow shells and provides a porcelainlike finish.

"Antique" eggshells have an old-fashioned design of flowers and twining leaves.

Snowflake patterns cut from folded tissue paper are glued on eggs dyed in assorted colors.

A variety of patterns created from circles and half circles. The designs are arranged to cover the holes at either end of the eggs.

Dyeing Eggs

Eggs to be dyed should be handled more carefully than those to be decorated without dyeing, since minute scratches invisible on a white shell may show clearly on a shell that is colored. If the shells need cleaning, wipe gently with a soft rag dipped in vinegar.

To dye the eggs, use commercial Easter egg dyes prepared according to package directions or add liquid food coloring to a half cup of water containing one teaspoon of vinegar. Since hollow eggs will not sink in the dyebath, they must be kept constantly in motion so that all parts of the shell are dyed an even color.

A few tricks can provide interesting effects. One is to dip part of the egg in melted paraffin before dyeing. The coated area will repel the dye, leaving a white area when the wax is scraped off or melted in a warm oven. The undyed portion can then be decorated with a tiny picture or made into a face.

Another resist effect uses tissue paper cutouts. Small shapes cut from white tissue paper are held in place against the eggshell by a layer of cheesecloth wrapped and tied tightly. After the egg is dipped in dye, the cheesecloth and paper cutouts are removed, leaving a mottled white pattern on the dyed surface. If colored tissue paper is used instead of white, the color will imprint itself on the shell, resulting in a two-color design.

A third type of dyeing uses the ink of the tissue paper to color the white surface of the egg, producing a delicate marbled effect. First a section of the egg is painted with water to which a small amount of white glue has been added. Torn shapes in different colors are then applied, and the glue-water mixture again painted on top. After a few moments (before the glue dries) the wet scraps are pulled off and discarded. Adding glue to the water helps make the transferred colors permanent—once dry they will not run when the next section of the egg is marbled.

Apply small tissue paper shapes to the egg's surface, dampening if necessary to hold in place. Wrap tightly in cheesecloth and dye.

Resist designs are white where tissue paper blocks the dye. Colored tissue paper produces a colored imprint.

Dye acts as a frame for a cheerful face made by dipping an egg in melted wax before dyeing.

To marble eggs, apply bright-colored torn tissue shapes with a mixture of glue and water.

Wait a few moments, then remove the still-wet tissue. Colors will run together where the papers overlap, creating a delicate "marbled" effect. When dry the colors are waterproof.

5

PAPER CUTTING

The silhouette is an ancient art form, with examples found in the Paleolithic cave paintings of France and Spain, the wall paintings of Egyptian tombs, and the graceful figures decorating Greek pottery. The Chinese were the first to apply silhouette techniques to paper, using the simplest of methods: they cut holes in light-colored paper so that the resulting stencil, when placed on a dark surface, would form a meaningful design. Among the earliest surviving examples of Chinese silhouette art is a paper cutting of a shrine, a thousand-year-old specimen discovered in the caves of western China.

As the art of papermaking spread to the West and paper became a cheap commodity, paper cutting developed as a form of folk art. In Poland the artist was the shepherd with his long shears, in Germany it was the farmer taking leisure from his fields, in Mexico it was the medicine man conjuring a lucky charm. Being of such lowly origin, the art was often ignored or disparaged: the word "silhouette," taken from the name of France's miserly minister of finance under Louis XV, was coined to denote the niggardly economy represented by the cheap black paper portraits popular in his day. To today's eyes, however, jaded as they are by the products of a mass-production society, paper cutting appears a vital and expressive art form.

Tissue paper, because it is so thin, is admirably suited for paper cutting. If secured firmly, up to fifteen layers can be cut at one time. This means either that a number of copies of a single design can be cut, or that one sheet of paper can be folded into parts and cut to produce a single intricate design.

This sinuous octopus, based on a painting found on a Minoan pottery jar, shows the Minoans' strong naturalistic sense. In the tissue paper rendition, the holes are cut using punches of graduated sizes.

Silhouette adapted from a Paleolithic cave painting. Early Stone Age man clearly recognized the visual impact of the silhouette.

A Polish paper cutting. Traditionally these were cut using long sheep-shearing scissors.

An ancient Chinese paper cutting depicting shrines decorated with monkeys, unicorns, phoenixes, and pigeons. Cut from light-colored paper, it is pasted on a dark background to accentuate the silhouette effect. One of the earliest paper cuttings in existence, this design dates back over one thousand years. *Photo courtesy British Museum*

Boy riding a porpoise. This would make a delightful illustration for a children's book. By Yumiko Tsukuda.

Cutting Duplicate Copies

When cutting a number of duplicate shapes from tissue paper, it is essential to keep the paper from slipping. The best method is to place a sheet of typing-weight paper under a stack of tissue paper, then cover the stack with a second sheet of typing paper on which the design is drawn. Staple all these layers together and they will hold firmly while being cut.

Any object to be decorated with a repeat pattern will make use of this method of cutting duplicate copies. But the technique has other uses as well. Lettering can be turned out in quantity, making tissue an inexpensive substitute for printing on posters and wall displays. Greeting cards can be produced in large numbers. Silhouettes, cut from a sketch or by casting the sitter's shadow on a wall, can be framed and sent to relatives as keepsakes. Finally, the cutout pieces can be exploited for their design potential alone. See, for example, the abstract pattern exercise on page 65, where a single abstract shape is combined in different ways to make a variety of patterns.

To keep layers of tissue paper from slipping, sandwich between sheets of typing-weight paper and staple through the whole stack.

A pair of good quality curved nail scissors makes intricate cuts more manageable.

Greeting cards using cut-paper designs based on Chinese motifs. About twelve copies of each design were cut at one time.

A single abstract pattern, cut freehand, is multiplied into a number of patterns.

A silhouette cut from a sketch. An alternative method would be to cast the sitter's shadow onto a wall, then use a pantograph (a mechanical tool available at art supply stores) to reduce the size of the image.

An old-fashioned frame gives an antique effect.

Cutting Folded Designs

Cutting folded pieces of tissue paper is another technique that takes advantage of tissue paper's thinness. A single piece of paper can be folded anywhere from halves to sixteenths, segments cut out, and the resulting shape opened to produce a symmetrical design.

Naturally, the way the paper is creased will affect the finished design. The simplest is to fold the paper in half, resulting in a symmetrical pattern repeated on each side of the central axis. For greater variation, the tissue can be folded in smaller segments. The series of diagrams on page 69 show a handy tool for producing 3- or 5-part folds. Cut out a replica in stiff paper or card, then use the 120° angle for dividing a design into 3, 6, or 12 parts, and the 108° angle for dividing designs in 5 or 10 parts.

To secure the folded layers while cutting freehand, staple around the perimeter of the design. When using a design sketched on typing paper, staple through those areas that are to be cut out. The more intricate the design, the more staples should be used to hold the layers in close alignment.

When the pattern is cut and unfolded, it will need flattening. This can be accomplished by using an iron at a low setting, or by pressing between the pages of a book.

Multiple-fold patterns cut freehand. The finished shape remains a mystery until the paper is unfolded.

Gift boxes decorated with cutouts. The tissue is glued to white shelf paper using spray adhesive.

Delicate medallions using naturalistic moifs. All are cut from paper folded in half. Four or five copies of each pattern can be cut at one time. By Yumiko Tsukuda.

A delicate pattern from paper folded in eighths. The center motif was cut after the paper was opened. By Yumiko Tsukuda.

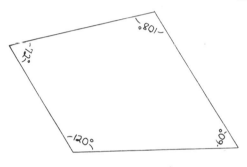

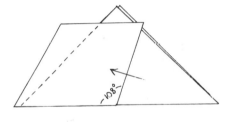

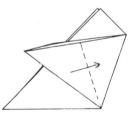

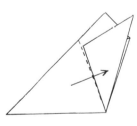

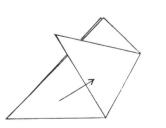

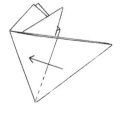

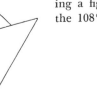

A scale for difficult folds. Cut the shape out of stiff paper or card and use as illustrated to mark the folding line. The 120° angle is for dividing a figure into 3, 6, or 12 parts; the 108° angle is for 5 or 10 parts.

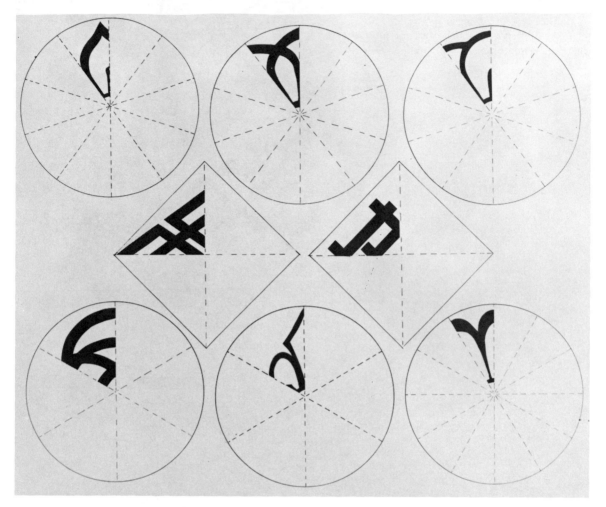

Japanese *mon,* or crests, are based on designs
cut from folded paper. Spaces to be cut out
should be stapled to hold the layers firmly.

Fastening Delicate Designs

Cutout designs in tissue paper are often exceptionally delicate, and great care is required in fastening them to a flat surface. If a cutout is to be framed under glass, it is easiest not to glue the whole design, but simply to secure it with a tiny dab of rubber cement and count on the pressure of the glass to hold the shape flat. If, instead, the design is to be exposed (as on a greeting card), the spray adhesive method illustrated in Chapter 2 is the most suitable. This method consists of picking up the fragile design on a sheet of stiff paper made tacky by a light coating of spray adhesive, then spraying the back of the design and smoothing it onto the desired background. A third technique uses laminating film to hold the tissue paper flat and in place. Lay the design on the backing paper, and cover with a piece of laminating film. When ironed according to the instructions in Chapter 2, the heat-sensitive surface of the laminating film will melt to bond the design firmly in place. The finished appearance is quite attractive, but, unless you have access to a laminating press that can handle large surfaces, the method is only suitable for small designs.

6

DECORATED PAPERS

Previous chapters have dealt with techniques for using tissue paper "as is"—that is, as it comes from the manufacturer. This versatile paper can, however, be decorated in a number of ways. This chapter deals with three of the most basic decorative techniques: fold and dye, stencil, and print.

Fold and Dye

There is an excitement in unfolding a piece of tissue colored by the fold and dye method, for, as more and more of the design emerges, a pattern totally unlike that of the original dyed segment is revealed. This multiplication of a single pattern into tens or hundreds invariably produces designs of great spontaneity—it is a process in which it is impossible to "go wrong."

There are two possible approaches to fold and dye. One—dipping the folded paper directly into liquid dyes—produces soft amorphous zones of color as the dye spreads itself through the absorbent paper. A second method—drawing with water-base felt pens on dampened tissue—gives a more controlled but equally decorative effect.

Either method calls for the use of absorbent white tissue paper. Avoid the slightly stiffened white tissue sold by the manufacturers of colored tissue paper; this has been treated in such a manner as to resist the dyes. Instead, choose the softer, less expensive wrapping tissue sold at variety stores.

Although variations are limitless, there are four basic ways to fold the paper for dyeing. The first is the simple accordion pleat. The other shapes start with the accordion pleat but are then folded to produce a square or rectangle, a right-angle or isosceles triangle, or an equilateral triangle. This last fold is the most difficult; it may require the use of a protractor to measure the first 60° angle. For unusual effects, experiment with irregular folds or with creases radiating from the center of the paper.

Four basic ways to fold tissue paper for dyeing: (a) accordian pleats, (b) squares or rectangles, (c) right-angle triangles, and (d) equilateral triangles.

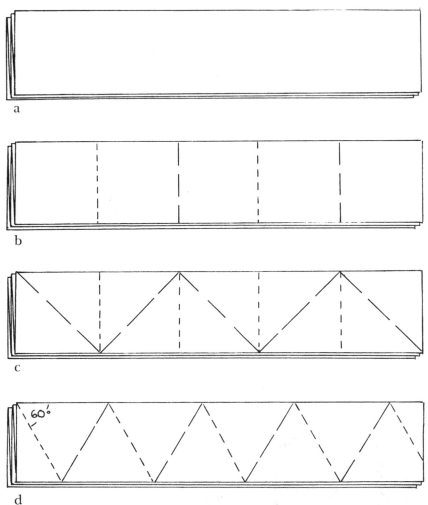

a

b

c

d

DIP-DYE

For the dip-dye method, use either liquid food colors or liquid water colors. The liquid water colors are preferable, since the colors are brilliant and a greater variety is available. Powdered dyes made up in concentrated solution are also suitable.

Pour the colors into shallow containers such as a teacup or cupcake tins. The colors can be used full strength, diluted with water, or blended together to produce different shades and intensities.

The process of dyeing is one of dipping and squeezing. Dip either the corner or the side of the folded paper into dye, allow the color to penetrate and spread naturally, then press the layers between newsprint or paper towels. This distributes the dye evenly through the layers and stops it traveling outward, thus allowing a certain control over the finished pattern. Dry tissue paper dipped in dye will produce a sharp-edged area of color; if a softer effect is desired, dip the folded paper in water either before or after dyeing one corner or side. Or dip just the tip of an already dyed but still damp corner into a darker color dye—the color will tend to travel along the folds, producing a starlike effect when unfolded. Still other variations can be achieved by allowing a design to dry, refolding on the same or different lines, and once again dyeing or dipping in water.

Dyes (food coloring and liquid watercolors) are assembled along with folded tissue paper to be dip-dyed.

The folded paper can be dipped in either water or dye. Dry paper produces a sharp-edged design; damp paper causes a softer effect.

Pressing the paper after each dipping stops the outward spread of the dye and disperses the color evenly among the layers.

Dip-dyed papers. The top papers were folded in squares, the middle in equilateral triangles, and the bottom two in right-angle triangles. Food coloring, liquid watercolors, and concentrated solutions of powdered dyes were used.

DYEING WITH FELT PENS

Dyeing with water-base felt pens is similar to dip-dye, except that after folding, the whole paper is dipped in water and the excess squeezed out. This dampness allows the water-soluble inks to penetrate a number of layers of paper. Draw a design on the top fold, then open to a fold where the ink has not fully penetrated and repeat the design. Continue working through the layers, reinforcng the design where necessary, until the bottom fold is reached.

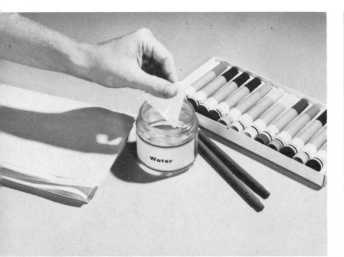

Before coloring with water-base felt pens, dip the folded tissue paper in water.

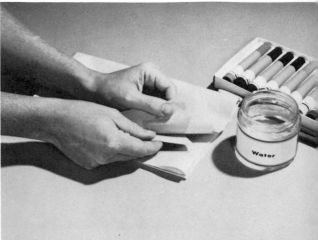

Squeeze out excess moisture between paper towels or newsprint.

Draw a design with narrow- or wide-tipped felt pens on the top of the folded and dampened paper. The moisture will cause the water-base inks to penetrate a number of layers.

Open to a point where the ink has not fully penetrated and go over the design. Repeat until the bottom fold is reached.

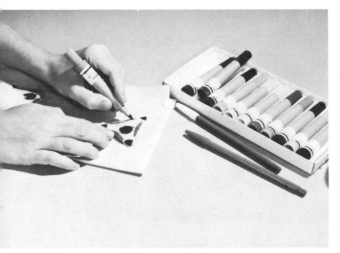

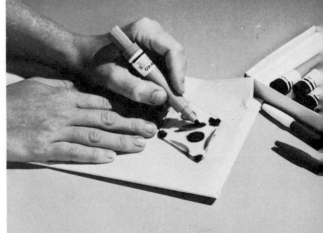

DRYING THE PAPER

To dry paper decorated either by the dip-dye or by the felt pen method, unfold only partway. While damp, the tissue is exceedingly fragile, and opening fully might cause the paper to tear. Instead, place the partially unfolded design between several layers of white tissue paper, cover with newsprint, and iron until nearly dry. The iron not only draws out the moisture; it also transfers some of the dye to the white tissue cover sheets, providing extra decorated strips that serve as attractive bookmarks. Unfold the tissue paper when it is nearly dry, and iron lightly with a warm iron to remove wrinkles.

Since these designs make use of water-based inks and dyes, they are liable to run if they come in contact with water. A coating of clear acrylic spray offers some protection. For a near-waterproof finish, paint with clear lacquer greatly diluted with lacquer thinner.

Papers decorated by the fold and dye method are often beautiful enough to frame and hang as they are, but they have other practical uses as well. They can serve as gift wrap, on greeting cards, to cover boxes, or as bookbinding papers. Because of the possibility of the color bleeding, they should not be used with water-based glues. Instead, use spray cement or apply with a warm iron using the waxy dry mounting paper discussed in Chapter 2.

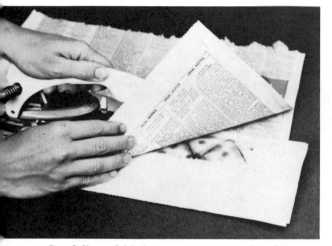

Carefully unfold the paper partway, place between several layers of clean white tissue paper, and cover with newsprint. Iron until nearly dry, then unfold and iron directly on the dyed paper to remove the creases.

The unfolded dyed paper and several "bonus strips" where the dye has penetrated the tissue paper.

Protect the dyed colors from running by spraying with clear spray acrylic or brushing with lacquer diluted with thinner.

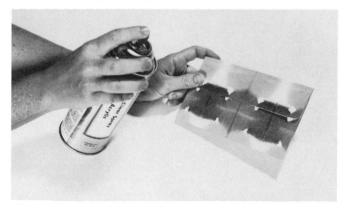

Colorful designs drawn with water-base felt pens. Narrow-tip pens are used for delicate designs.

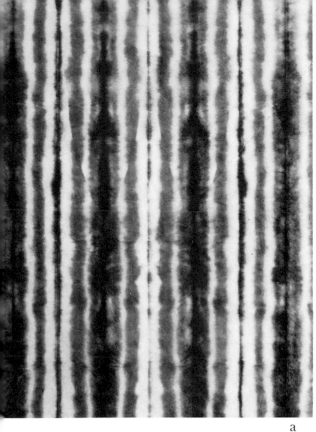

a

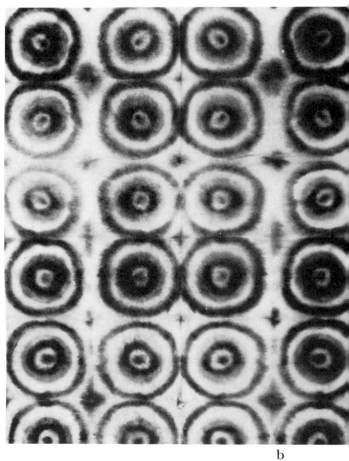

b

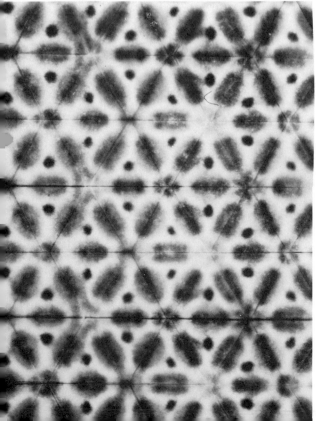

c

Designs drawn with wide-tip felt pens. The folds are (a) accordian pleats, (b) squares, (c) equilateral triangles.

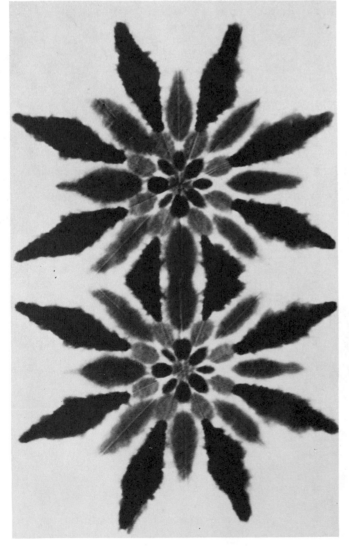

Felt pen designs radiating from a center fold.

Dip-dyed paper used to decorate greeting cards and envelopes. The paper is secured with iron-on dry mounting tissue.

Gift wrap folded from full sheets of tissue paper and dyed with felt pens. To use, wrap a package first with white shelf paper, then cover with the decorated tissue.

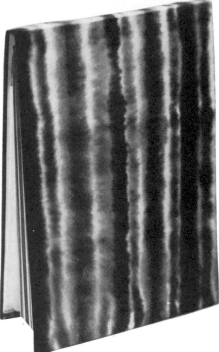

Note pads and address books covered with felt-pen-dyed tissue paper. Use spray adhesive or iron-on dry mounting tissue to adhere the tissue paper to a white backing sheet, then use this reinforced paper to cover the notebooks.

Decorated boxes. Use iron-on dry mounting tissue to attach the decorated paper to 2-ply bristol board, then cut and fold into box shapes.

Stencils

A stencil is a handy device for applying a repeat pattern to the surface of colored tissue paper. Three types of stencil-decorated papers are illustrated here. In the first, transparent dye sprayed from an aerosol can supplies the color. In the second example, the designs are sprayed on with ordinary enamel paint. Then the process is reversed, and bleach is used to remove color from the stencil-cut area.

For all three applications, the stencil is cut in the same manner. Stencil paper, a stiff, waxy material, can usually be found in art supply stores; if unavailable, use any stiff paper. First cut out the design using scissors or a stencil knife. Cut around the design, leaving about a two-inch margin, and secure the stencil to a larger piece of paper in which an opening the size of the stencil area has been cut. This larger sheet will serve as a cover sheet to protect the tissue paper from overspray. Finally, spray the surface of the stencil *very lightly* with spray adhesive and invert the sprayed surface, including the covering sheet, onto the tissue paper to be decorated. The spray adhesive serves to keep the stencil in close contact with the tissue paper so that there is no leakage of paint. Finally, spray a light coating of transparent dye or enamel, then lift the stencil and reposition it in the next area to be decorated.

To bleach out an area, dip a toothbrush in bleach, and draw a knife blade over the bristles to create a spatter effect. Watch closely as the color lightens, and halt the bleaching when it reaches the desired stage by dabbing the tissue paper with a paper towel.

Stencils made by spraying transparent dye through a design cut in stencil paper.

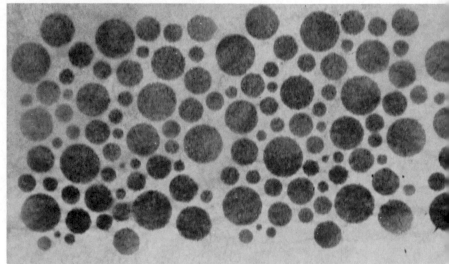

Enamel in spray cans is applied to tissue paper. For gift wrapping paper, gold spray paint is especially effective.

Mask the stencil with newsprint to prevent over-spray, then coat the stencil lightly with spray adhesive.

Press the tacky surface of the stencil face down on the tissue paper to keep it from shifting, then spray lightly with enamel.

Bleach spattered on with a toothbrush removes the color from the stenciled areas.

A second method is used with objects that cannot be gripped in the hand for printing: leaves and grasses, lace, feathers, etc. A rubber roller is used to spread block printing ink over the face of a piece of glass or other hard, nonabsorbent surface. The object to be inked is laid face up on newspaper, and the inked roller is pressed over the surface, coating it evenly. The object is then placed, inked side down, on the tissue paper, where it is pressed either by hand or with a clean roller to make an imprint. A layer of newspaper or a sheet of foam rubber placed under the tissue paper will make the imprint more distinct.

Let your imagination roam when making stamp or roller prints. Often the most everyday items—a wooden spool, an apple sliced in half, a lettuce leaf—can be used to create an intriguing design. Given the fact that tissue is one of the least expensive papers available, this is an extremely economical way of creating hand-designed wrapping paper.

Cut gum erasers with a stencil knife, press on a pad saturated with ink, dye, or poster color, and stamp the design on the tissue paper.

Printing

Two basic types of printmaking are especially suitable for use with tissue paper. One, a stamping method, uses a felt or foam rubber pad saturated with ink, dye, or poster color. For the stamp, objects such as nails, buttons, and kitchen utensils can be used, or the design can be cut from a sliced potato or from an art gum eraser. The surface to be printed is simply pressed on the ink pad, then stamped on the tissue paper.

Eraser prints. Slight irregularities in cutting and painting add charm.

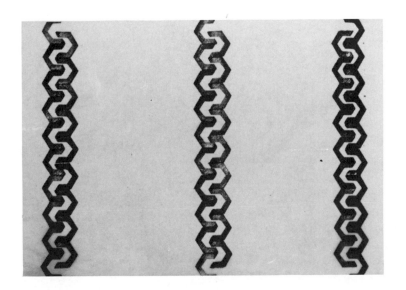

Christmas tree decorated with paper roses.

Boxes decorated with designs cut from tissue paper.

Folded tissue paper stars act like stained glass when held to the light.

Honeycomb fruits fold flat when not on display.

"Stained glass" sun. Layers of tissue paper are embedded in polyester resin.

Shadow puppet jester of tissue-covered acetate.

Decorative papers made by dipping folded tissue paper in colored inks and dyes.

Children's fort of foam core board decorated with tissue paper.

Fruits and vegetables. A panel for the kitchen.

Multifaceted boxes can be assembled to make a variety of designs.

Easter eggs. The tissue paper design appears hand painted.

Word cards labeled with transfer lettering and covered with adhesive-backed plastic film.

Repeat designs made by drawing on damp, folded tissue paper with a felt pen.

Lilies. An example of Japanese paper folding.

A field of pink paper daisies.

Imaginary flowers in an assortment of colors.

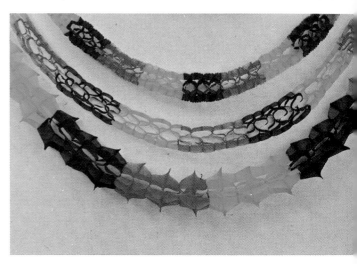

Three garlands cut from a single stack of glued tissue paper.

Topiary tree with flowers cut from two-sided laminated tissue paper.

Colorful garland made by glueing tissue paper in layers.

Christmas tree lights made of crushed tissue paper shaped around small balloons.

"Stained glass" animals of polyester resin coated with tissue paper.

Shadow puppets. Tissue paper is applied to shapes cut from clear acetate.

Roses of laminated tissue paper in a dried flower arrangement.

Candles with tissue paper designs embedded under a layer of wax.

Canister covers of braided tissue paper.

The Christmas tree is actually a roller leaf print. Block-printing ink is applied to the leaf using a rubber roller, then the leaf is pressed onto the tissue paper.

7

COLLAGE

The word "collage" comes from the French verb *coller,* to glue or stick. Although the technique of making pictures from glued elements is an old one, it was not until artists like Picasso and Braque began to incorporate tangible objects in their paintings that the idea began to attract attention. Their work in the early 1900s inspired a flurry of experimentation that ultimately led to collage becoming a recognized art form.

Although virtually any material can be incorporated in a collage, paper—especially transparent paper—has always held an attraction for artists working in the medium. Tissue paper, with a range of colors as

varied as those of the artist's palette, is especially suitable. It can be torn, crushed, folded, layered, or combined with other materials and still retains its transparency and brilliance.

Commercially dyed tissue can naturally be used in collage, but many artists prefer to color their own papers. One of the reasons is permanence: commercial tissue paper cannot be expected to resist fading to the degree that hand-colored papers can. A second motive is variety: when the artist is in control of the dyeing process, a wide range of effects can be achieved. Some of the possible coloring techniques are discussed in this chapter.

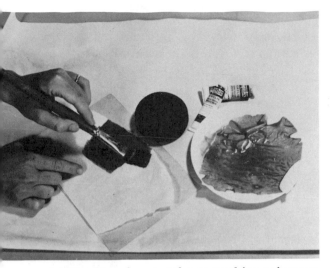

Artist's watercolors or polymer emulsion paints can be used to "paint" tissue paper. Thin the pigment with water, then let the tissue paper soak up the color in a shallow dish, or brush the color directly onto the paper.

Coloring Tissue Paper by Hand

PAINTED PAPERS

Both artist's watercolors and polymer emulsion paints can be used to "paint" tissue paper. Watercolors offer pure, transparent color, but papers dyed with watercolors are not completely lightfast, and they may run when they come in contact with a water-based glue.

Polymer paints * are the best choice for producing colored papers that are both waterproof and resistant to fading. These paints consist of pigments suspended in an emulsion of synthetic resin and water. (Since acrylic is the synthetic resin base most widely used, they are often referred to as acrylic paints.) Although they can be thinned by the addition of water, polymer paints dry to a strong, waterproof bond.

* Liquitex (U.S.), Hyplar (U.S.), and Cryla (U.K.) are well-known brands.

One method for applying either artist's watercolors or polymer paints is to thin the pigment with water in a shallow dish or pan, then allow a piece of white tissue paper to absorb the color. Another is to place the absorbent white tissue paper on a waterproof surface such as glass or acetate and brush on the thinned pigment. Do not allow tissue colored with polymer paints to dry in contact with any other surface or the paper will stick: the medium in which the pigments are suspended consists of a very strong adhesive, the same one that is often used (see below) in assembling collages.

DYED PAPERS

When paints are used as the coloring agent, the pigments may tend to cloud the paper's transparency. If it is desirable to preserve tissue paper's full transparency, dyes are recommended instead.

Water-soluble aniline dyes probably offer the most brilliant color range, but it is worthwhile experimenting with various fabric, craft, and even Easter egg dyes. Make a concentrated solution of the dye in water following the manufacturer's directions, and pour this into a large, shallow tray. If dyeing just a few sheets of paper, a baking tray is perfectly adequate. Since spills may be difficult to remove, it is a good idea to cover the work area with newspapers or a plastic cloth, and to wear rubber gloves when dyeing.

To dye, fold a piece of absorbent white tissue paper into halves or quarters, depending on the size of the tray used, and immerse in the dyebath. Folded paper is less apt to tear when wet, but if the folds are too numerous, the dye will tend to collect along the creases, giving an uneven result. When the color has penetrated fully, lift the paper gently and allow the excess dye to run back into the tray. Without unfolding, lay the damp paper on folded newspaper to dry. The color may lighten somewhat as the tissue dries; if a more intense hue is desired, the dyebath can be strengthened.

It is a good idea to dye a large quantity of paper at one time, and to keep a good assortment of colors on hand for use when the need arises.

Immerse white wrapping tissue in a shallow dyebath. Use a concentrated solution of aniline dye, or experiment with other fabric, craft, or Easter dyes.

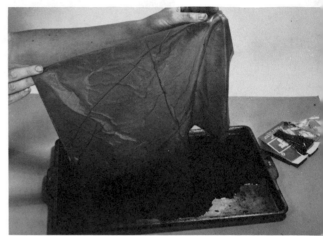

Lift the paper gently to avoid tearing, and allow excess dye to run back into the dyebath.

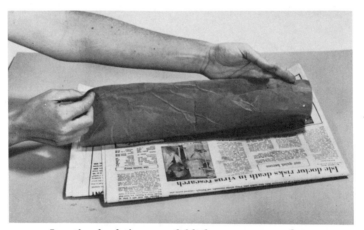

Lay the dyed tissue on folded newspaper to dry.

MOTTLED PAPERS

Interesting effects can be achieved by combining different colors in a single piece of paper. Virtually any water-based coloring material—liquid watercolors, thinned polymer paints, concentrated dye solutions, vegetable colors—can be used. Depending on the nature of the paint or dye chosen, the colors may be permanent or they may run and blend further when incorporated into a collage using a water-based adhesive.

To make mottled paper, place a sheet of white tissue on a nonabsorbent surface such as glass or acetate, and apply the dye or paint using an eyedropper or paintbrush. Water can also be splashed on to cause the colors to run more freely. Add additional sheets of paper and repeat the process, then separate the layers and allow them to dry. In this way a number of sheets of paper, each different from the other, can be created at one time.

An even easier method, especially suitable for schools, is to use commercially-dyed tissue to make mottled paper. Simply splash water on a piece of colored tissue paper, and cover with a second color paper. Since the dyes run freely when wet, the process can be continued indefinitely until the desired quantity of mottled paper is produced.

Splash on water to make the colors blend more freely.

Cover with a second sheet of tissue paper and add more color and/or more water. Continue until the desired number of sheets are colored, then separate the layers and allow them to dry.

Use water-based colors to mottle tissue paper. Place absorbent white tissue on a sheet of glass or acetate, and use a paintbrush or eyedropper to apply color.

Examples of mottled paper.

MARBLED PAPERS

Paper colored by any of the techniques described above can also be marbled to produce interesting variations. Marbling relies on the incompatibility of oil and water: oil-base colors will float on the surface of a water bath, and the flowing design they produce can be imprinted on a sheet of paper lowered onto the water's surface.

The only materials required are a shallow pan of water, oil colors, turpentine, brushes, and containers for mixing the colors. Oil-base felt pen inks can be squirted directly from the can, but other oil colors require thinning so that they will spread freely over the surface of the water. Mix oil paints with enough turpentine (preferably high-quality artist's turpentine) to make the paint runny but not thin. Pour the color directly from the jar onto the surface of the water, or hit a loaded paintbrush against the side of the pan to spatter the color. Swirl the water or break into the design with a stick to produce interesting pattern variations. If the initial results are unsatisfactory, vary the quantity of turpentine used or try adding a little varnish to the oil-turpentine mixture.

When ready to print, lower the tissue paper onto the surface of the water. If one side of the paper contacts the water, only that surface will be printed. If the paper is submerged in the water bath, a second and different design will be imprinted on the other side of the paper. Whichever method is chosen, remove the paper immediately after it is printed and spread on newspaper or hang from a clothesline to dry.

"Fern Grotto" by Nelda Fagothey. An abstract collage made entirely of hand-dyed and marbled papers glued over gold wrapping paper. A nonglossy finish is achieved by mixing wheat paste and white glue.

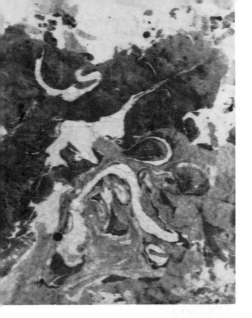

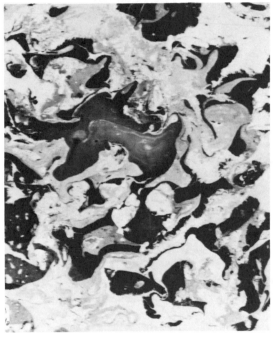

Examples of marbled paper created by squeezing drops of color from cans of oil-base felt-pen ink onto the surface of a water bath. Different brands have different flowing characteristics, so experiment with several types.

Paper marbled using oil colors. Thin oil paints with artist's turpentine, then pour or splash onto the surface of a water bath. Allow marbled paper to dry thoroughly before incorporating in a collage.

BLEACH

Interesting effects can be produced by removing color rather than adding it. When household bleach is dripped, spattered, brushed, or printed on the surface of colored tissue paper the portion contacted will turn white. The pattern produced can be controlled to a certain extent by keeping a paper towel handy to blot up excess moisture and keep the effect of the bleach from spreading too far. If a paintbrush is used to apply the bleach, be sure to choose an old or discardable one, since animal hair is greatly harmed by the disintegrating effects of the bleach.

The accompanying photograph shows just one of the effects possible when printing with bleach. A cellulose sponge was dipped in diluted household bleach, squeezed nearly dry, and applied to the paper. All the irregularities of the sponge's surface appear with perfect clarity.

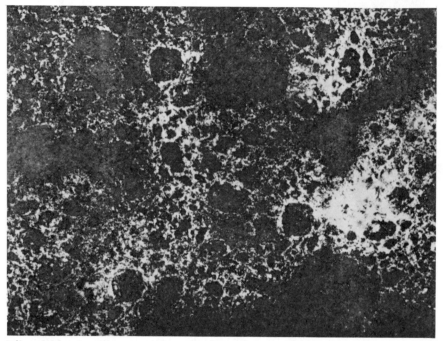

Diluted bleach will remove the color from tissue paper. Brush or spatter it on, or use objects such as a cellulose sponge to print a pattern on the paper's surface.

WAX

A crackled effect can be produced by crushing tissue paper, dipping in melted paraffin or candle wax, and spreading it out on a flat surface. A paintbrush is used to force dye or bleach into the cracks, producing a pattern of fine lines. The paper is then ironed between sheets of newspaper to remove the wax.

A star-burst shape can be created by twisting tissue paper into a point, dipping the point in melted wax, and applying bleach to the waxed area once the paper is spread flat.

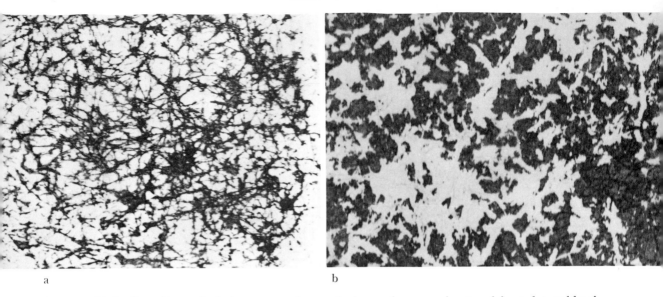

a   b

For a crackled effect, dip crushed tissue paper into melted wax, then spread out and force dye or bleach
into the cracks. Dye is used in example (a); bleach in example (b). When dry, iron the tissue between
sheets of newspaper to remove the wax.

A starburst effect created by dipping twisted tissue paper
into melted wax, spreading flat, and brushing bleach out
from the center of the waxed area.

Collage Techniques

GROUNDS

Once you have assembled a supply of dyed and colored papers, you can begin thinking about putting a collage together. The first problem is deciding what ground, or support, best suits your needs.

Untempered hardboard is one of the most widely used grounds for collage.* Rigid and lightweight, it resists warping and readily accepts the adhesives used in applying tissue paper. Plywood, though heavier and more cumbersome, also provides a rigid backing.

Canvas board and stretched canvas also make suitable grounds. If already primed, no further treatment is necessary before beginning the collage.

Paper can be used for experimental collage or for work in schools, but since it tends to buckle on contact with water, it should be avoided for any work of a permanent nature. Rather more suitable are the heavier paper boards such as mat board and Upson board, both available at art supply stores.

PRIMERS

Treated canvas or canvas boards and white-surfaced papers need no priming, but other porous or nonabsorbent surfaces (untreated canvas, plywood, hardboard) require a coating so that adhesives will stick to them. Primers, generally white, have a secondary function of providing a luminous surface that will show up transparent papers to the best advantage.

Gesso, a creamy substance incorporating chalklike material such as gypsum, sulfate of lime, whiting, or zinc white, is the primer most generally chosen by artists. Polymer gesso, an improved product with

* Masonite, Weldwood, and Presdwood are well-known trade names.

a synthetic base, is especially suitable for flexible surfaces such as stretched canvas. Ordinary white latex house paint is a cheap and often employed substitute for gesso.

To apply, stir the primer thoroughly and thin to a creamy consistency if necessary, then simply brush on as you would any paint. If a heavier coat is called for, use two thin coats rather than one thick one. The primer dries quickly; under normal conditions it should be dry and ready to work within an hour.

ADHESIVES

Polymer emulsions are the adhesives most widely employed by artists working in the field of collage. White and creamy, they consist of emulsions of synthetic resins suspended in water. Although they can be thinned with water, they behave like plastics, drying to a strong, clear, waterproof finish.

Polymer medium (also known as acrylic medium when the synthetic base used is an acrylic resin) is especially favored because of its permanence. This is the same substance in which pigments are suspended to make polymer or acrylic paint. Manufactured to artist's specifications, it is noted for its high quality and ability to resist yellowing, cracking, and other signs of aging. Polymer medium is thin enough to be applied with a brush; if a more paste-like adhesive is preferable, gel medium (a pure, unthinned polymer emulsion) can be substituted.

White glues such as Elmer's and Sobo are similar to polymer medium and only slightly inferior in quality. Generally of a polyvinyl acetate rather than an acrylic base, they behave exactly like polymer medium in that they can be mixed with water but dry to a clear, waterproof finish.

Because of a difference in acidity, however, the two types should not be mixed.*

Both polymer medium and white glue dry to a glossy finish. If the gloss is objectionable, the effect can be diminished somewhat by thinning the glues with water or, in the case of polymer medium, by choosing the mat variety marketed by several companies. Another alternative is to combine one of the emulsion glues with wheat paste (generally purchased in powdered form from art suppliers or wallpaper dealers). Wheat paste can also be used alone for an attractive nonglossy finish, but for reasons of permanence and flexibility it is usually mixed with white glue or polymer medium.

Other adhesives—rubber cement, spray glue, mucilage, paste—can be used experimentally for creative effect, but in general they should be avoided in any work considered permanent.

PROCEDURE

The first step in assembling a tissue paper collage is to plan the nature of the design by arranging cut or torn shapes of tissue paper on the chosen ground. Parts can be shifted and added or taken away until a satisfactory arrangement is found.

When ready to begin glueing, pour out the needed amount of adhesive into a small container. If using white glue, thin it with enough water to reach proper brushing consistency. Gels and pastes may be brushed on, or they can be spread with a palette knife. Any brush will do for applying adhesive, but nylon brushes, especially de-

* Neither should different brands of polymer medium be used together. Some (Liquitex, Cryla) have an acrylic base, while others (such as Hyplar) are copolymers (acrylic and vinyl).

signed for use with polymer paints, are by far the easiest to clean.*

Begin by spreading glue over the area where the paper is to be pasted. Lay the paper in place, and brush over the top with a second coating of glue. In this manner the paper is not only adhered to the ground, it is also covered with a coating that will dry to a clear protective film. Continue adding pieces of paper until the design is complete, then brush on a final coating of polymer emulsion to act as a protective varnish.

Collages made using one of the polymer emulsions should not be framed under glass. There are two reasons for this: first, the emulsion coating itself offers more than adequate protection, and second, the glass may stick to the surface of the collage. This is because the emulsion coating, even if perfectly dry to the touch, retains an adhesive quality if subjected to pressure. If for some reason it is essential to use glass, always include a mat or spacer of some sort to keep the collage and glass separated.

* Dried polymer adhesive can often be removed from nylon by soaking the brushes in warm water, but animal hair brushes will require treatment in solvents such as acetone or lacquer thinner to loosen the dried glue.

Plan a design by arranging cut or torn tissue paper shapes on the chosen ground. Note how overlapping shapes produce new colors.

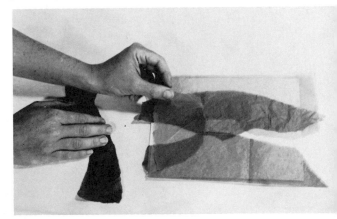

Brush glue liberally over the area where the paper is to be applied.

Lay the tissue paper in place, and brush over the tissue paper with a second coat of glue. Emulsion glues dry to a clear, waterproof film.

"Carp" by Gloria H. Lane. Scraps of gold foil are used to suggest the reflective quality of the water and to illuminate one of the fish. The artist uses white glue as adhesive and mat polymer medium as a final varnish.

Color can be added before a collage is begun or while it is in progress. Some inks and dyes will blend freely with the water-based glues, others (such as artist's drawing ink) may react with the adhesive to create unusual patterns.

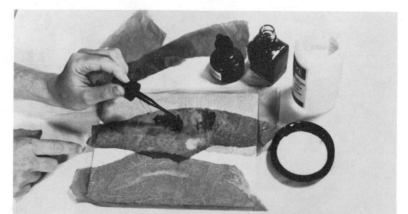

Carolyn Hiatt uses pen and ink to define the animal shapes in her collages for children. She chooses canvas board as a backing and frames the collages under glass, including a mat to keep the glass separated from the surface of the collage.

Additional Techniques

REFLECTIVE BACKING PAPERS

A collage of tissue paper acquires a luminescent quality when a reflective backing is substituted for the traditional coat of white primer. Gold and silver wrapping papers, either dull or shiny, make an interesting surface from which to begin a collage. The paper can be used flat, or, for a textural quality, crushed and glued down. For an even more reflective surface, experiment with aluminum foil or some of the mirror-finish gold and silver acetates.

UNDERPAINTING AND OVERPAINTING

Many artists choose to apply a color wash to the ground before beginning a collage using tissue paper. The color serves to accent certain areas of the design or to unify the work as a whole. Inks, dyes, or paints

can be used. Polymer or acrylic paints, because they are compatible with the polymer medium favored as an adhesive, are widely chosen.

The application of color can continue while the work is in progress. If a piece of tissue paper appears unsatisfactory when glued in place, it can be overpainted with an acrylic wash. Colored inks or liquid watercolors can be brushed or dropped from an eyedropper onto the surface and allowed to flow into the areas still wet with adhesive. Depending on the compatibility of the adhesive and the coloring material chosen, the colors may blend freely or may react in unusual ways.

Some artists use additional color to provide structure for their designs. In her collages for children Carolyn Hiatt uses pen and ink to outline the animals' shapes and to accent details such as flowers and leaves. Acrylic paints are employed by Honolulu artist Gloria Foss to define the trunks and branches of trees in her collage "Foster Gardens." Similar results can be achieved by drawing over a design with felt pens, pastels, crayons, rubber stamps, or any other suitable material.

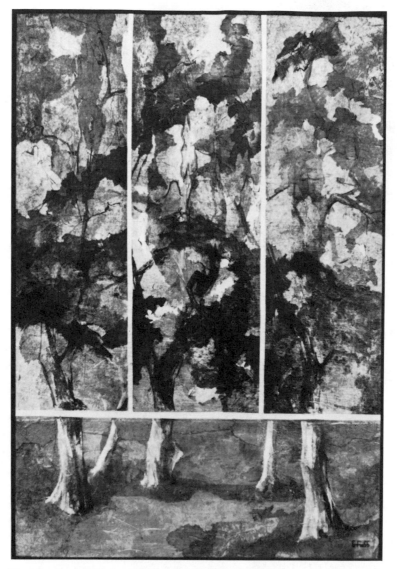

"Foster Gardens" by Gloria Foss. Silver backing paper provides a luminescent quality. The artist hand colors her paper with aniline dyes, and uses acrylic paints to accent and define details of the design.

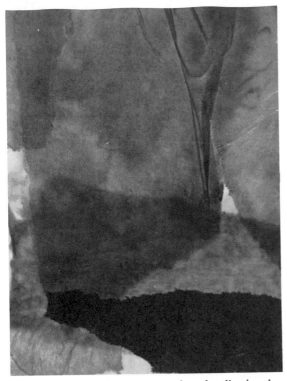

Liberal use of water or water-based adhesive induces color bleeding. Note the soft effect produced on the left-hand side of the collage by removing a piece of tissue paper after its color has transferred to the backing sheet.

BLEEDING TISSUE PAPER

Lift a piece of tissue paper that has been placed on a sheet of wet paper and you will find that the dye has imprinted itself on the surface. This technique can be used to provide colorful backgrounds for designs in media such as pen and ink or charcoal. Or it can be used to create a subtle wash of color as the basis for beginning a collage. If a little white glue or polymer medium is mixed in with the water used for bleeding the tissue, the colors will dry waterproof and will not run when coated with subsequent layers of adhesive.

There may be times when the bleeding that is characteristic of commercially dyed tissue paper is undesirable. If this is the case, it helps to coat the paper on both sides with spray acrylic. Glue the paper using as little water in the adhesive as possible, and allow each piece of tissue paper to dry before adding the next.

TISSUE PAPER AND PRINTED MATERIALS

Because of its transparency, tissue paper can be used quite successfully as a color wash over such printed materials as newspapers, posters, magazine clippings, and book jackets. A single layer adds the enlivening effects of color without interfering with the legibility of the print. The color also has a unifying effect, and can be used to draw discrete elements of a design into a single, satisfying whole.

Tissue paper can be used to add color and unity to a collage incorporating printed materials.

TEXTURED EFFECTS

The natural tendency of tissue paper to wrinkle when wet can be used to advantage in tissue paper collage. The paper can either be applied flat to a wet surface and encouraged to wrinkle with a brush loaded with adhesive, or it can be rolled or crushed beforehand and then secured by brushing adhesive both underneath and on top of the paper. Veining can be further accentuated by the addition of water-based inks or paints. The color tends to travel outward along the creases, emphasizing the paper's textural quality.

"Hibiscus" by Ute Kersting. Textual interest is provided by veining and crushing the paper. Tissue paper and Japanese handmade papers are used together in this collage.

"Out of Darkness" by Elisabeth A. Mears. White latex paint is used to prime the plywood backing board. The hand-dyed tissue is applied using a mixture of white glue and wheat paste, and the completed collage protected with a coat of varnish.

THREE-DIMENSIONAL EFFECTS

Many elements can be incorporated in a tissue paper collage to produce a three-dimensional effect. Sand, string, cloth, lace, or netting can be secured with polymer emulsion to add surface interest. Acrylic modeling paste, polymer gel, spackle, or other such materials can be built up with a palette knife. The effect desired may be abstract, or the relief materials may be used to suggest three-dimensional forms such as mountains, waves, or buildings.

Tissue paper plays an important role in collages that incorporate relief materials. It has the advantage of adding color without obscuring textural detail. More important, it can be used to unify elements of a design that might otherwise be lacking in cohesiveness.

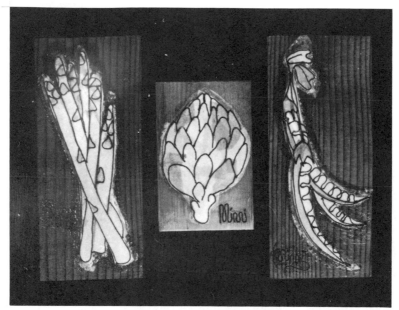

A collage technique is used to apply tissue paper to raised shapes cut from cardboard and glued to wooden plaques. Black string outlines the vegetables. By Carolyn Hiatt.

COLLAGE FOR SCHOOLS

Tissue paper collage is an exciting medium for school-age children. Not only can students experiment with placing the paper shapes before glueing them, they can also observe the effects of colors bleeding and mixing with one another when a water-based glue is applied. The tissue paper itself is very inexpensive, and, if economy is a primary concern, white glue can be used instead of polymer medium and drawing paper substituted for rigid grounds such as hardboard or canvas board.

Tissue paper collage can also be used in conjunction with block printing. Youngsters can manage traditional single-color prints, but multicolor effects requiring the cutting of two or more blocks are generally considered beyond the scope of the beginner. Collages of tissue paper, however, not only make colorful backgrounds for block printing; they also can be glued in such a way as to make it appear that the color is not pasted but applied in separate printings.

This technique was developed by a Honolulu schoolteacher, Frankie Morris, to introduce her fifth and sixth graders to multiple-color printing. She had her students attach a sheet of tissue paper to a white backing sheet, with the aim being to achieve a splotchy rather than an evenly glued effect. A second sheet was applied over the first, again leaving some spots unglued. The result was an apparent color separation, with a different color showing through in the glued and unglued areas. When a design cut from linoleum block was printed on top of the tissue paper, the finished work had the look of a three-color print.

A block print on tissue paper has the appearance of a three-color print. Two colors of tissue paper are glued to a white backing, then printed in a third color with a linoleum block. By a sixth-grade student.

Tissue paper is used to differentiate ground and sky in this block print.

Cut and torn tissue paper shapes are used as a background for a block print in light-colored ink.

8

PAPER FLOWERS

Paper flowers can fill a room with vibrant color, brightening the darkest corner. Economical and easy to make, they can be produced in abundance in a minimum of time. Although nature may provide the initial inspiration, imagination is an even more vital ingredient—rather than mimicking actual flowers, paper flowers are at their best as a whimsical or zany interpretation of the real thing. The possible combinations of color and shape are infinite—this chapter merely introduces some basic techniques and provides instructions for a few examples.

Flower Stems

Wire comes in a number of thicknesses or gauges, with numbers 12 to 24 being the most suitable for use with paper flowers. Twelve- or 14-gauge wire is rigid and heavy —it is best used for the stems of very large flowers. Eighteen or 20 gauge is of medium weight—an all-purpose wire. Numbers 22 and 24 are lightweight—suitable for small flowers or curving stems. In addition to straight lengths, finer (approximately 30 gauge) spool wire is useful for fastening petals to the stem wire.

Both straight and spool wire can be purchased plain or with a cotton covering. Cotton-covered stem wire is a convenience, for wrapping the wire is made unnecessary. White cotton-covered wire can also be painted or dyed in a variety of colors.

Flower stems do not necessarily have to be made from wire. Cane or wooden dowels are picturesque with large flowers. Wooden knitting needles make a combination stem and flower center when threaded with tissue paper petals; long straight pins topped with a bead can be used in the same way. Finally, an interesting effect is produced by wiring flowers directly to a wooden branch or even to a living plant.

Flower Centers

Commercial flower stamens are available in a wide variety of shapes and sizes, but they can also be made by hand. One method consists of starching embroidery thread, cutting it into appropriate lengths, and dipping the ends into a mixture of white glue and powdered poster color. For variety, the still-damp stamens can be dipped into poster color powder or in flocking to give the impression of pollen.

Fringed tissue paper also makes a colorful flower center. Fold a long, narrow strip of tissue in half lengthwise (fold two strips together for a multicolor effect) and fringe with scissors. Make a crook in a piece of stem wire, and draw it through the fringed paper to make sure it cannot slip. Then wind, glueing the base of the fringe, until the desired fullness is reached.

A third alternative is to curve the end of a length of stem wire over a ball of cotton, then cover with tissue paper for a rounded flower center. This can be left as it is, or wound with thread to divide the center into equal parts.

Wind embroidery thread back and forth around nails set in a backing board and brush with a mixture of white glue and liquid laundry starch.

When dry, lay the stiffened strings across strips of cardboard coated with double-faced adhesive tape. Cut each row to the desired length.

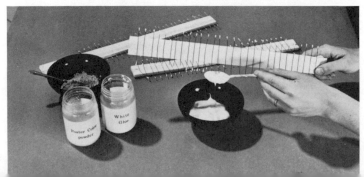

Use the cardboard strip to hold the stamens while dipping the ends in a mixture of white glue and powdered poster color.

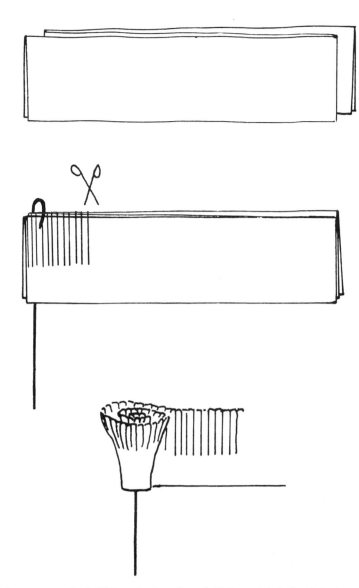

Fold a strip of tissue paper in half lengthwise, then fold into thirds for fringing. Slash the folded edge with scissors at even intervals, then draw a piece of stem wire with a crook in it through one end of the fringe. Wind, using dabs of glue to secure the base, until the desired fullness is reached.

Assembling the Flower

Once the flower center is complete, add the flower petals, using glue or spool wire to secure. White glue or clear model cement are suitable, but rubber cement, which remains sticky rather than drying, is not recommended.

In most cases you will want to wrap the flower base and stem to cover unsightly bulges and messy ends. For best results use commercial floral tape or strips of crepe paper cut across the grain. Both are available in a wide assortment of colors. The floral tape is self-adhesive, but crepe paper requires small dabs of glue to keep it in place. As you wind, pull the tape or paper taut to ensure a smooth finish. Leaves cut from tissue, crepe paper, or construction paper can be inserted as the tape is being wound.

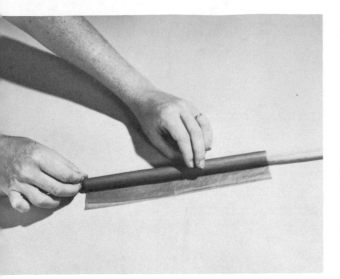

To crepe tissue paper by hand, first roll the paper loosely around a wooden dowel or other round object.

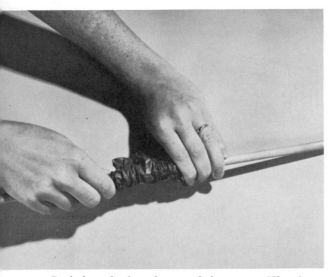

Push from both ends toward the center. The tissue can be pulled off, flattened, and used as it is, or it can be rolled and crushed again to produce finer creases.

To crepe tissue by the handkerchief method, fold two or three petals in half and place inside a handkerchief. Hold the palm of one hand on the base of the petals, and use the other hand to pull the cloth firmly away from the center crease.

Unusual Effects

Tissue paper can be treated in a number of ways to provide interesting effects. One of the most attractive is to crepe the paper by hand, producing a fresh crinkled effect much different from the machine-made creases of commercial crepe paper. The easiest method is to roll tissue paper loosely around a round object—anything from a pencil for small flowers to a broomstick for large ones. Then use both hands to push the paper toward the center. Unwrap the paper and use as is, or spread it out gently and repeat the rolling and crushing to produce finer creases. The tissue can be treated in this manner either before or after the petals are cut. A colorful variation can be created by fastening two sheets of tissue paper together with spray cement, then cutting and creping the petals. The result is a flower with petals of two different colors.

A second way to crepe paper is the handkerchief method. Here the petals are cut, folded in half lengthwise, and placed inside a handkerchief or other light material. Using the palm of one hand to hold the base of the petals, the cloth is pulled firmly away from the center crease. Since the tissue paper is fragile, care is necessary to avoid tearing it; it helps to treat several petals at the same time.

There are also methods to make the petals glossy. Spraying with lacquer or clear acrylic is the easiest, but for a shinier effect try dipping the finished flower in thinned lacquer or in heavily catalyzed polyester resin (see Chapter 13 for instructions on using plastic resin). Flowers dipped in lacquer become almost transparent; those dipped in plastic resin, which is of a heavier consistency, assume an almost glasslike appearance.

Wax can be used to make petals translucent without rendering them transparent. Melt candle stubs or kitchen paraffin in a double boiler over hot water (because it is inflammable, the wax should not come in direct contact with the heat source). Dip the finished flower into the wax, lift and gently shake off excess droplets, and allow to harden. For a shinier effect, dip the flower briefly in cold water immediately after removing it from the hot wax. Handle the completed flower carefully to avoid cracking the wax coating.

Flowers

PARTY FLOWERS

These flowers can be made very quickly in almost any size. Stack five or six squares of tissue paper and fold as indicated in the diagram. Fold the resulting square in half and cut the top in a curved line. Staple the base, then open out the layers one by one. Tape firmly to a wooden dowel or strong wire.

Instead of cutting curved petals, the folded shape can be fringed to make small chrysanthemumlike flowers to decorate gift packages.

Party Flowers in bright pinks and oranges.

Valley fold on the lines indicated by short dashes, and mountain fold on the diagonal indicated by long dashes.

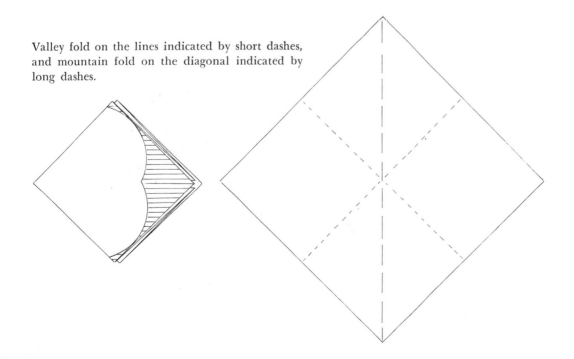

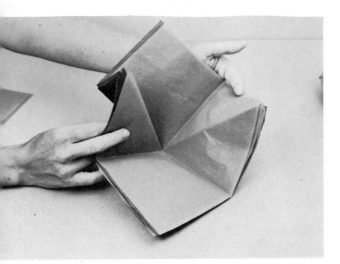

Once the paper is creased, bring the corners into the center.

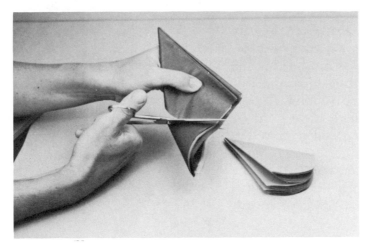

Fold in half and cut the top in a semicircle.

Staple at the base and open out the layers one by one.

Miniature Party Flowers bloom in pots on a gift package.

A bouquet of fringed Party Flowers decorates a gift box.

113

BUTTON CHRYSANTHEMUMS

Fold a strip of tissue paper in half without creasing, and cut slashes along the folded edge. Open and reverse the fold, placing the paper over a wooden dowel to round out the petals. Fold the strip in thirds lengthwise, and wind around a wire bent down at the top. Use white glue along the base of the fringe to hold in place.

Button Chrysanthemums.

Fringe a strip of tissue paper, then reverse the fringe over a wooden dowel to round out the petals. Wrap and glue around a length of stem wire, stopping when the desired fullness is reached.

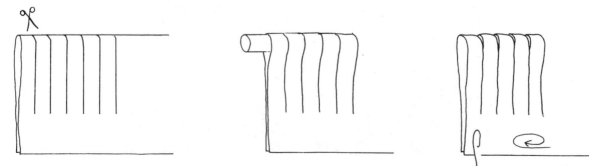

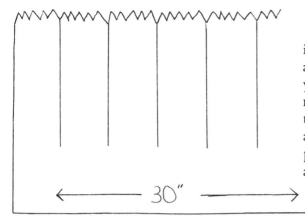

← —— 30″ —— →

Cut a 30-inch strip as indicated, and add a
second strip if necessary for greater fullness.

CARNATION

Cut a 30-inch strip of tissue paper as
indicated in the diagram, and wrap around
a length of wire, gathering at the base as
you go. Add a second strip if greater fullness is needed. Wrap the stem with floral
tape or crepe paper cut across the grain,
and insert leaves cut from construction
paper. To curl the leaves, draw them over
a knife or scissor blade.

A pink Carnation.

SIXTEEN-PETAL FLOWER

Cut eight petal shapes as indicated in the diagram. Loop spool wire through the middle of a bunch of stamens, then use this wire to join the petals in groups of two. Secure the spool wire to a length of stem wire, and wrap with floral tape or crepe paper.

Sixteen-petal Flower in white with black stamens.

Cut eight petal shapes and use spool wire to gather the petals in groups of two. Secure to a length of floral wire and wrap the stem with floral tape or strips of crepe paper.

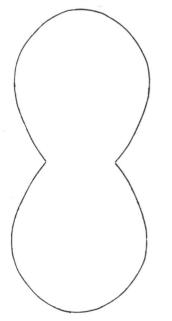

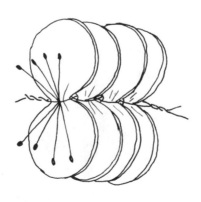

DOUBLE-PETAL FLOWERS

For each flower cut two petal patterns and fold as indicated. Do not crease the folds. Twist the base and add a spot of white glue to maintain the shape, then wire into a bouquet or glue to a ring cut from cardboard for a wreath or candle ring. Cut leaves from double crepe paper made by joining two sheets with spray cement.

(Below) A candle ring of Double-petal Flowers in light and dark pink. The leaves are cut from a double layer of crepe paper joined with spray glue.

Use two petal shapes for each flower, and fold without creasing.

For a wreath or candle ring, glue flowers and leaves to a circle cut from cardboard.

STRAW FLOWERS

Make a ½-inch flower center of black fringed tissue paper as explained in the section on Flower Centers. Wrap this with about ⅛ inch of yellow fringed tissue to accentuate the flower center. For petals, make slashes in a long strip of brightly colored tissue about 1½ inches wide. Wind and glue this fringe around the flower center until the desired fullness is reached.

Straw Flowers in brilliant shades of pink, orange, green, and blue.

PLEATED FLOWERS

Stack four layers of tissue paper approximately 3 by 5½ inches and make accordion pleats down the center of the strip. Wire the center firmly and fluff out each of the layers. For a vibrant effect, alternate layers of different colored tissue paper.

Pleated Flowers.

Make accordian pleats down the center of a stack of tissue paper. Wire the center and fluff out the layers.

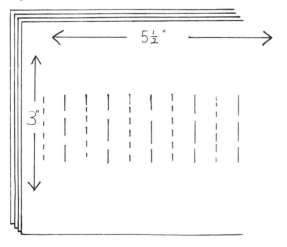
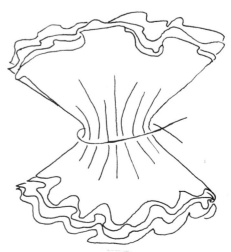

A field full of pink Daisies.

DAISIES

Make a flower center by looping stem wire over a small ball of cotton and covering this with a circle of colored tissue paper. Thread two of the petal shapes onto the wire and glue to the flower center, crushing the base slightly to give added shape. When petals are threaded onto the stem in this manner a neat finish results, and there is no need to wrap the stem with tape.

Cut two pattern shapes for each flower and thread onto the stem wire. The flower center is made by covering a ball of cotton with a circle of tissue paper.

CIRCLE FLOWERS

Make a cut to the center of a circle of tissue paper, then curl by drawing the flower over a scissor blade. Slide a length of white cotton-covered stem wire through the center of the curled shape and fasten with white glue at the base of the flower.

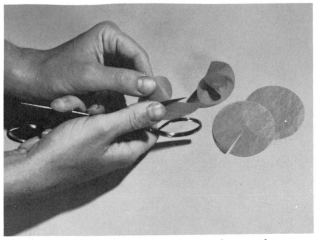

Cut each circle to the center, then curl over the blade of a pair of scissors.

A mass of flowers shaped from circles of tissue paper.

COSMOS

Make a flower center of dark purple
fringed tissue paper, then thread a single
flower pattern onto the stem and glue at
the base. Choose colors such as pink, rose,
light purple, and white.

Cosmos.

Make a center of fringed tissue paper, then thread
a two-inch diameter petal onto the wire.

HALF-MOON FLOWERS

Use five or more circles for each flower. Fold each circle in quarters, creasing only the second fold. Glue the folded shape to a length of stem wire, and place a dab of glue inside the creased section to hold the fold in place. Glue five such shapes around the wire.

Half-moon Flowers.

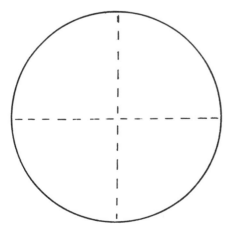 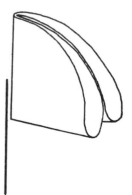

Fold a circle of tissue paper in quarters, creasing only the second fold. Glue five or more folded shapes around a length of stem wire.

Bachelor Buttons in bright blue have flower centers of light and dark blue.

BACHELOR BUTTONS

Make a fringed flower center using two colors of tissue paper. Thread three pattern shapes onto the stem wire, and glue around the flower center. It is not necessary to wrap the stems.

Cut three pattern pieces for each flower.

FOLDED ROSES

Fold a strip of tissue paper in half without creasing, and wrap loosely starting at one end. Gather at the base and wrap tightly with spool wire.

To make a rose tree, poke holes in a Styrofoam cone, and insert the wired base of each rose into a hole, using white glue to hold in place. Use smaller roses toward the top of the tree.

A Rose Tree made by inserting flowers in a Styrofoam cone base.

Fold a strip of tissue in half without creasing, roll loosely, and wire firmly at the base.

PARTY ROSES

Cut two long strips of tissue paper in deep scallops, then wind and glue around a length of stem wire. Roll tightly at the center, then more loosely toward the outer folds. Gather the base and secure with spool wire, then wind with floral tape or strips of crepe paper. These large roses are especially effective made in two colors, such as light and dark pink, or yellow and orange.

Party Roses.

Wind and gather two strips of scalloped tissue paper around a dowel or heavy wire.

For small roses, cut folded paper in scallops, unfold, and wind, gathering at the base.

CABBAGE ROSE

Crepe each petal on two sides by winding loosely over a wooden dowel or broomstick and pushing from the ends toward the center. Wrap one petal tightly to make the flower center, then continue adding petals until the desired fullness is reached. Wire the base tightly to hold the petals in place.

Cabbage Rose.

Crush both sides of each petal over a wooden dowel.

Yardstick Roses.

YARDSTICK ROSES

Wind a strip of tissue paper several times over a flat ruler or yardstick, and crepe by pushing the ends in toward the center. Leave an inch or two unwrapped, and use this margin to wind up the flower from one end. Wrap the base tightly with spool wire, then cover with floral tape or strips of crepe paper.

Wrap tissue several times around a flat ruler leaving an inch or two margin, and crush toward the center.

Insert a wire and wrap from one end.

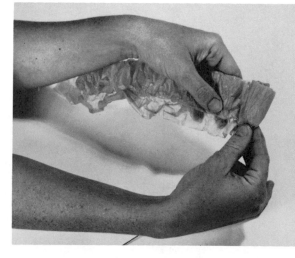

CURLICUE FLOWERS

Wind a strip of tissue loosely over a wooden dowel, leaving a margin of about one inch unwound. Crepe the paper by pushing inward on both ends, then carefully remove the dowel. Keeping the unwound portion on the inside, wrap up the flower from one end and fasten tightly with spool wire. Wrap the stem to conceal the wired base.

Curlicue Flowers.

POSIES

Cut a rectangle from hand-creped tissue paper, then twist at the center and fold in half. Assemble four such petals along with a single stamen and wire together over a length of stem wire. Cover the stem with floral tape or strips of crepe paper.

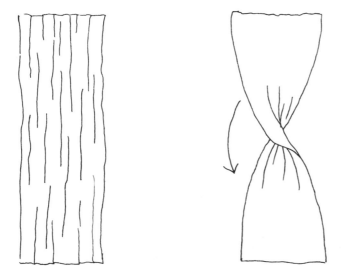

Make four petals of crushed paper as shown and wire together over a length of stem wire.

Posies in a miniature basket.

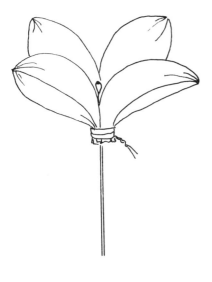

SWEET PEAS

Using hand-creped tissue paper, fold two circles together as shown, and pass a length of spool wire along the fold. Draw the ends of the wire together and twist to hold, then shape the flower by drawing the front three petals forward. Fasten to flexible stem wire with floral tape, and arrange in a bouquet. Add some curled tendrils for a realistic effect.

An arrangement of Sweet Peas with characteristic curled tendrils.

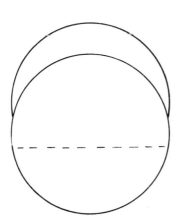
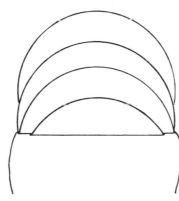

Use spool wire to shape two folded circles of hand-creped tissue paper.

LILIES

Use spray cement to glue together two sheets of tissue paper of contrasting color. Cut as indicated, then crepe the petals by rolling over a wooden dowel and crushing. Wrap around a length of stem wire, and insert stamens made by wrapping thin wire with tissue paper. Wrap with floral tape, inserting leaves cut from a double layer of green hand-creped tissue.

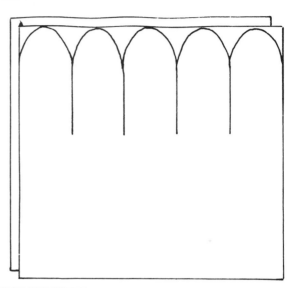

Glue two sheets of tissue paper together with spray cement, then cut as indicated and crepe the petals.

Lilies made from two-color paper have a contrasting color on the underside.

PEONY

Cut eight of each of the three petal shapes, and crepe by the handkerchief method discussed under Unusual Effects. Dye cotton-covered wire to match the tissue or wrap flexible wire with tissue strips and glue to the center back of each petal. Use twisted strips of tissue paper for the flower center, and assemble the petals starting with the smallest and working outward. Add leaves of double-layer creped tissue.

Cut eight of each pattern shape.

Peony. Each leaf is shaped by folding in half and crushing by the handkerchief method.

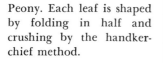

Poppy.

POPPY

Make the flower center by covering a ball of cotton with tissue paper and wrapping with embroidery thread. Surround with stamens, then add petals that have been creped by the handkerchief method. Wrap the stem with floral tape or strips of crepe paper.

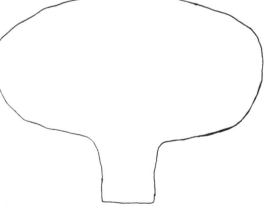

Use five or six petals for each flower and crepe by the handkerchief method.

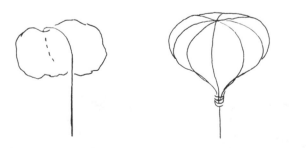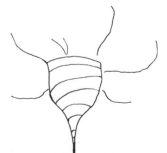

CHRYSANTHEMUM

Fold a long strip of tissue paper in half lengthwise and fringe the unfolded side. Keeping the two layers together, draw a dowel or pencil end down each petal, exerting enough pressure to cause the paper to curl. Starting from one end, wrap the curled petals around stem wire and secure with glue or spool wire when the desired fullness is reached.

Chrysanthemum.

Fringed petals can be curled by drawing the end of a dowel or pencil (without eraser) down each strip.

9

JAPANESE PAPER FOLDING: ORIGAMI

The word "origami" comes from the Japanese verb *oru* (to fold) and the noun *kami* or *gami* (paper). Although it is not clear where in the Orient paper folding originated, the tradition is most firmly established in Japan, where for centuries folding figures from a square piece of paper has been a favorite children's pastime. Due to its growing popularity, the craft now claims international recognition, and new folds are contributed each year by craftsmen around the world.

Although paper folding may at first seem difficult, proficiency is less a matter of skill than of practice. Most figures rely on a limited number of basic folds; once these are mastered, the designs that can be created are virtually limitless. The folds presented here, chosen because they are decorative and relatively easy, are but a small number of those in existence. Those wishing to explore origami more thoroughly should consult the works listed in the bibliography at the back of the book.

Origami is a disciplined craft, requiring both precision and accuracy. Individuality can, however, be introduced in a number of ways. Varying the size of the paper used, combining two sheets of different colors, adding a decorative frill, or modifying indicated cuts are all means of adding an individual touch.

For neat folds, it is important to start with a perfectly square sheet of tissue paper. Although at least one manufacturer sells tissue cut into squares, the shapes are not regular and cannot be used without trimming. It is not difficult to cut squares if a sheet of graph paper is used as a guideline. Staple the graph paper securely to a stack of tissue (use the staples liberally to prevent slipping), then cut using a sharp stencil knife and a metal-edged ruler for guidance.

The folds used in origami are tradition-ally known as "mountain" and "valley" folds, names that graphically describe the manner in which the paper is creased. In the diagrams that follow, short dashes are used to indicate a valley fold, and long dashes to indicate a mountain fold. An arrow describes the direction of the fold, while a diagram of open scissors indicates a cut. The steps have been made as explicit as possible, but do not be discouraged if they seem troublesome at first. Once a fold is mastered, reproducing it will become second nature, and soon it will no longer be necessary to refer to the diagrams.

Staple graph paper to layers of tissue paper to provide a guideline for cutting perfect squares. Use scissors or, preferably, a stencil knife to cut through the layers.

MOUNTAIN

VALLEY

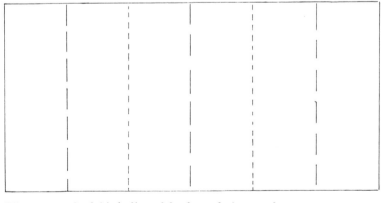

The mountain fold, indicated by long dashes, and the valley fold, indicated by short dashes, are the two basic origami folds.

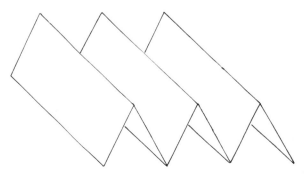

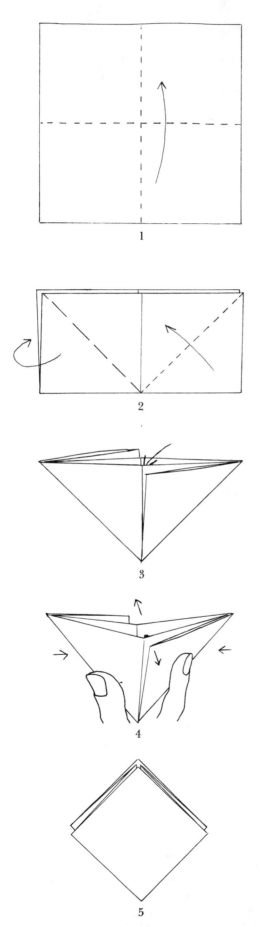

BASIC FLOWER FOLD
1. Fold the paper in half vertically, then open. Fold the bottom half up to meet the top.
2. Mountain and valley fold as indicated.
3. Open the figure from the center.
4. Push in the sides and open out the center following the direction of the arrows.
5. Basic Flower Fold step 5. A number of shapes can be folded from this figure.

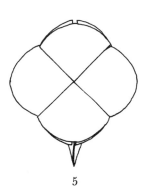

1

2

3

4

5

BASIC FLOWER FOLD—variation 1

1. Start with Basic Flower Fold step 5. Fold the top flaps to the center.
2. The figure will look like this. Turn it over and repeat step 1 on the back.
3. Cut along the line indicated.
4. Hold at the dotted line and pull out the four petals.
5. The completed flower.

A bouquet using Variation 1 of the Basic Flower Fold. A fringe is added to the center of each flower.

The same flowers used in a wall plaque. By Tomoko Ito.

1

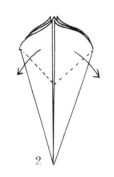

2

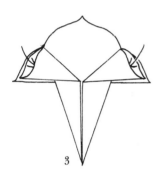

3

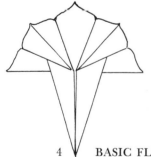

4

5

Other variations can be created by altering the cutting line.

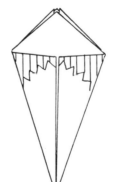

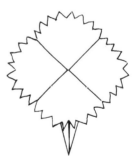

BASIC FLOWER FOLD—VARIATION 2

1. Fold as for Variation 1, but cut in the shape indicated.
2. Fold the top flaps down along the dotted line. Turn the figure over and repeat on the back.
3. Insert a pencil or finger where the arrows indicate and open out the folds.
4. Flatten the opened folds. Turn over and repeat on the back.
5. Variation 2 has eight petals instead of four. Add a decorative flower center if desired.

Variation 2 of the Basic Flower Fold.

Lilies. These are folded using two sheets of tissue paper in contrasting colors. A felt pen adds the characteristic spotting.

142

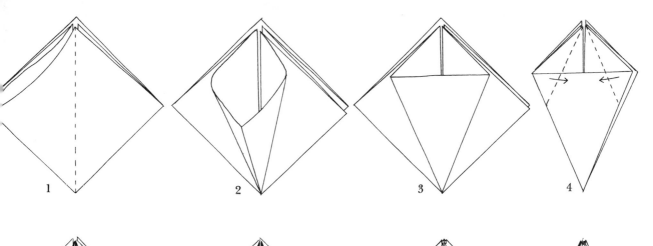

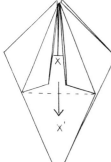

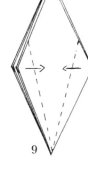

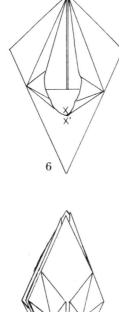

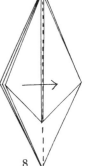

LILY

1. Start with step 5 of the Basic Flower Fold. Valley fold on the dotted line and begin opening the top flap.
2. Open the flap fully and press it flat.
3. The figure will look like this. Turn over and repeat with the three remaining flaps.
4. Valley fold on the dotted lines, bringing the top flaps to the center.
5. Open the flaps partway and pull out and down from point X.
6. Continue pulling downward until X meets X' and the fold is pressed flat.

7. The figure will look like this. Repeat on the three remaining sides to reach step 8.
8. Valley fold on the top layer as indicated.
9. Valley fold on the dotted lines, bringing the sides to the center.
10. The figure as it looks now. Repeat step 9 on all four sides.
11. The completed fold. Roll each of the petals down over a pencil or wooden dowel to curl.
12. The lily. Cut leaves from construction paper and curl by drawing over a scissor blade.

1

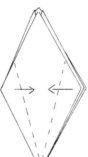

2

3

4

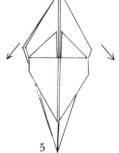

5

6

Iris in three shades of purple. It is based on a modification of the lily fold.

IRIS

1. Start from step 8 of the lily fold. Bring the flap up, following the arrow. Repeat on all four sides.
2. Fold the top flap along the dotted line.
3. Valley fold along the dotted lines, bringing the sides to the center. Repeat on all four sides.
4. Fold the front flap down; turn and repeat on the back.
5. Pull out and down on the two side flaps.
6. The completed flower.

A bouquet of miniature Cube Flowers.

The same flowers arranged on a single stem.

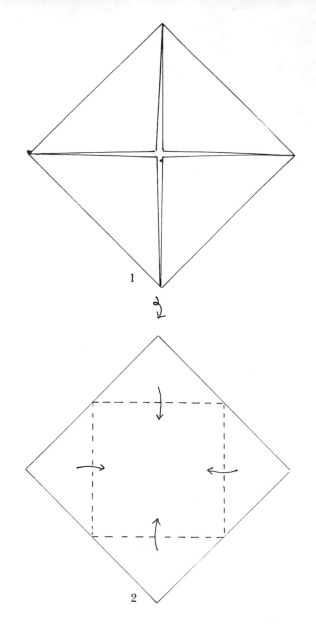

1

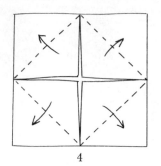

4

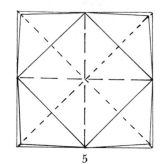

5

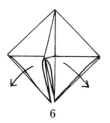

6

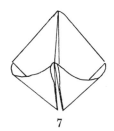

7

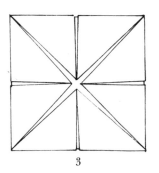

3

CUBE FLOWER

1. Fold the four corners to the center.
2. Turn the figure over and again fold the four corners to the center.
3. The resulting figure. Reverse again to reach step 4.
4. Fold the four flaps outward along the dotted lines.
5. Valley and mountain fold on the lines indicated, at the same time pushing the center up from below.
6. The resulting figure viewed from the side. Open out the four pockets.
7. Glue the bottom tips together to hold the flower's shape.

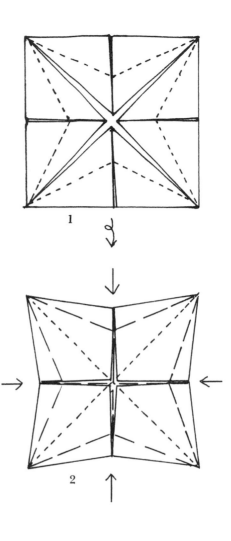

A variation of the Cube Flower.

CUBE FLOWER—A VARIATION

1. Start with step 3 of the Cube Flower. Make valley fold creases along the dotted lines.
2. Turn the figure over. Make valley and mountain folds along the lines indicated. Press inward in the direction of the arrows, at the same time pushing the center up from below.
3. A side view. Open out each of the four petals.
4. Glue the bottom tips together to hold the flower's shape.

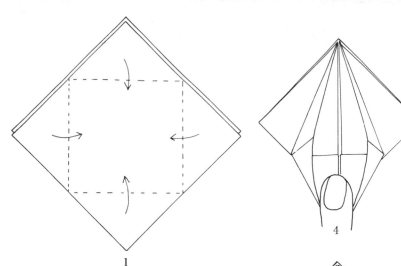

1

7

4

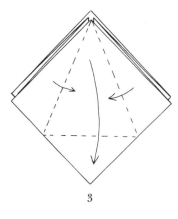

2

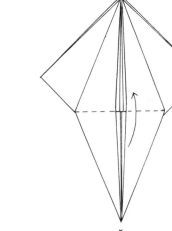

5

STAR ORNAMENT

1. Use two sheets of paper of contrasting color. Fold the corners to the center.
2. Follow steps 1 through 5 of the Basic Flower Fold.
3. Crease the top flaps by folding the sides into the center. Open partway, then pull the top flap down in the direction of the arrow.
4. Pull down until the fold is flat to reach step 5.
5. Fold up along the dotted line.
6. The figure as it now looks. Repeat steps 3 through 5 on the three remaining sides.
7. The completed fold. Grasp the two middle points and pull out and down.

3

6

A star-shaped ornament is folded from two sheets of tissue paper.

Glue six Star Ornaments at their tips to make a hanging ball.

An intricate-looking Christmas ornament made by joining six identical origami figures. If made in a large enough size, the ornament can accommodate a small light bulb. Light glowing from inside shows up the folds to great advantage. By Yasuko Tomi-yama.

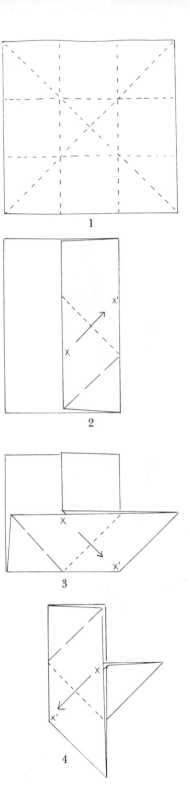

1

2

3

4

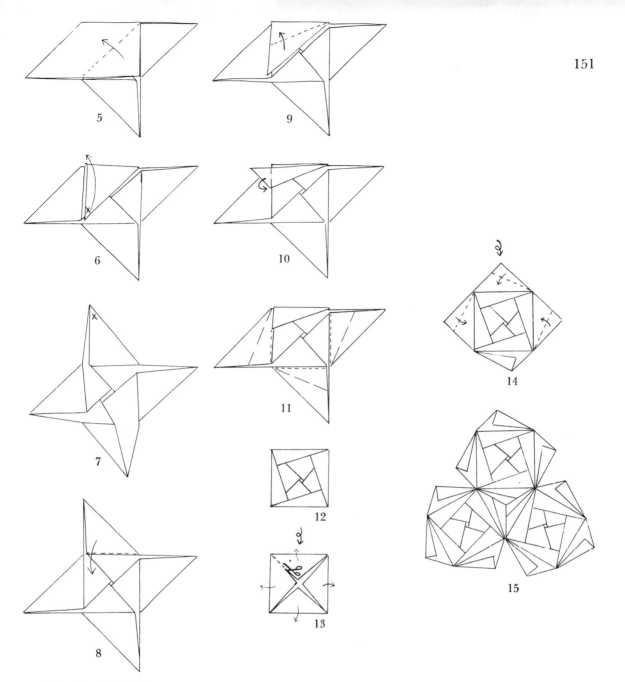

CHRISTMAS BALL

1. Use two sheets of paper in different colors. Crease along the dotted lines as indicated, then fold the right-hand third of the paper across the center to reach step 2.
2. Make valley and mountain folds as indicated, bringing point X to meet X'.
3. Repeat the valley and mountain folds on the second side, again bringing X to meet X'.
4. Repeat on the third side.
5. Crease by folding along the dotted line.
6. Open the figure enough to release point X. Pull this out until it matches the position of the three other points.
7. Flatten the figures.
8. Fold along the dotted line.
9. Fold up the flap as indicated.
10. Tuck in the point behind the front layers.
11. Repeat on the three remaining sides.
12. The figure as it now appears. Turn it over.
13. Cut open the back of the figure as indicated and open out the flaps.
14. Turn the figure to the front again and fold the opened flaps as shown.
15. Attach three shapes together by glueing the folded flaps. Six shapes joined in this manner will make a Christmas ball.

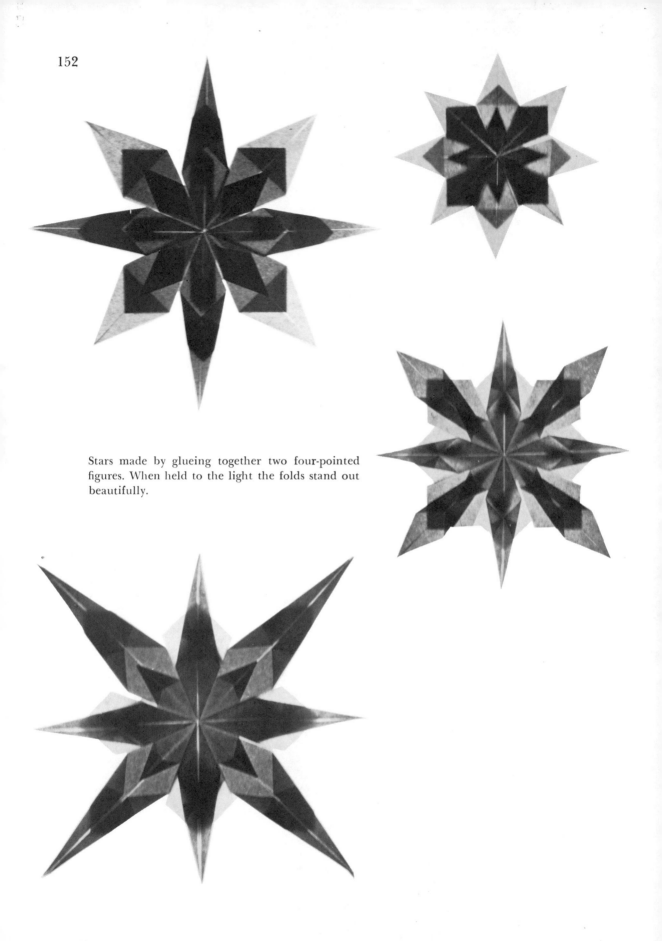

Stars made by glueing together two four-pointed
figures. When held to the light the folds stand out
beautifully.

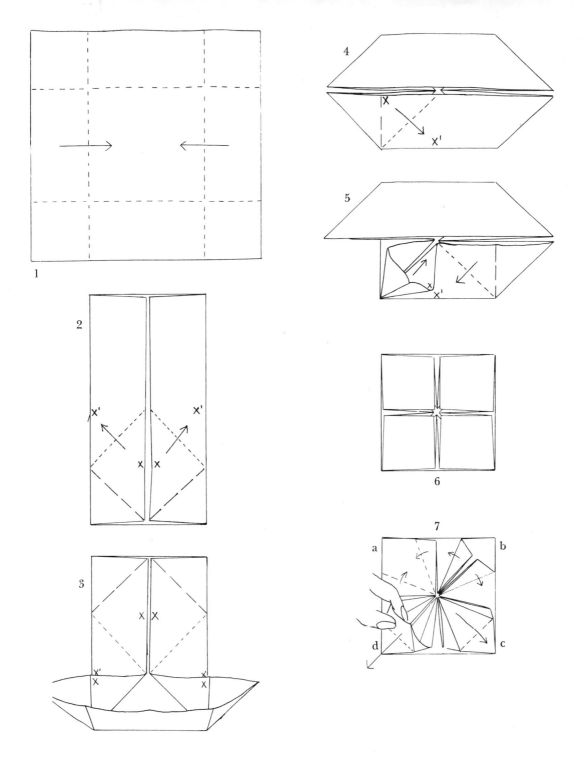

STAR

1. Crease as indicated, then fold the left and right sides to the center.
2. Mountain and valley fold as indicated, bringing points X to meet X'.
3. Flatten the fold. Repeat step 2 on the top half of the figure.
4. Mountain and valley fold along the lines indicated, bringing X to meet X'.
5. Flatten the fold by bringing the corner to center. Repeat on the three remaining sides.
6. The fold as it now appears.
7. Four steps are illustrated. Start in the upper left-hand corner.
   a. Fold side flaps to center as indicated.
   b. Open flaps.
   c. Pull out and down from center.
   d. Continue pulling out and down until the fold is flat.

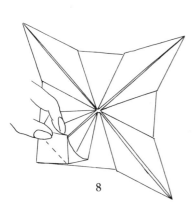

8

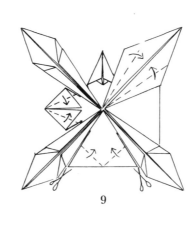

9

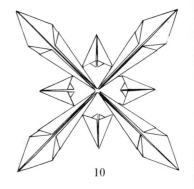

10

8. Repeat until all four sides are opened out into a star. The star shape can be left as is or modified. Steps 9 and 10 show one variation.
9. Start in the upper right-hand corner.
   a. Fold sides to center along the dotted lines.
   b. Make cuts as indicated two-thirds of the way to the center. Fold the cut flaps as indicated.
   c. Fold the flaps once again to center.
   d. The fold will look like this.
10. The completed figure.

10

DECORATIONS

Tissue paper is, above all, a decorative material. Its vibrant colors bring life to the darkest room. Thin and flexible, it can be cut, shaped, or folded into shapes ranging from lacy chains to geometrical solids. Since it is inexpensive, it can be used lavishly whenever a striking impact is needed. Whatever the occasion—a dance, a festival, or a seasonal celebration such as Christmas or New Year's—tissue paper decorations will help to enhance the party atmosphere.

Certain qualities make decorations particularly effective. They should be bold and eye-catching in order to stand out from the competing background. Properties of scale must be considered—a small mobile might be lost in a ballroom, while a bunch of giant flowers could dwarf a luncheon table setting. Finally, a sense of unity in the overall design is important: a limited number of colors and shapes will have a greater decorative impact· than an indiscriminate combination of unrelated designs.

Decorations from Pleated Paper

It is surprising how a technique as simple as pleating paper can be adapted to produce a wide variety of designs. Pleated paper can be shaped into a chain, opened into a star, or cut into a dainty snowflake.

Although pleating is a basic skill that requires little explanation, one simple folding trick helps speed the process considerably. Instead of folding randomly, try folding the tissue along with a sheet of graph paper. First crease the graph paper in the desired intervals, then flatten it out and lay on it the tissue paper to be folded. Starting at one end, refold the graph and tissue paper together. The procedure is not only efficient; it produces sharp creases of near-perfect regularity.

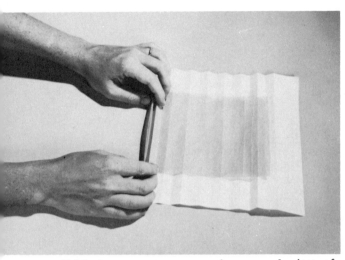

Fold tissue paper on top of a creased piece of graph paper to reproduce accordian pleats of uniform size.

Pleated shapes in pink, orange, and green are joined end to end to form a chain.

The same chain pulled into a circle.

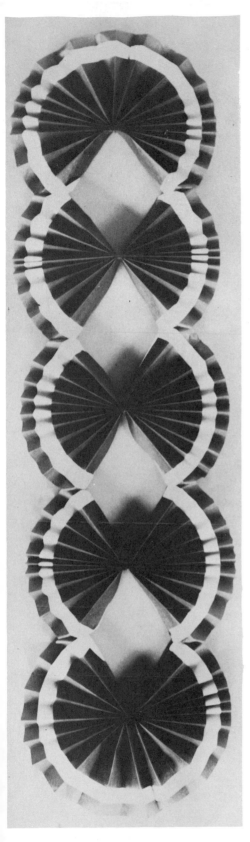

Three layers of tissue paper in red, white, and blue are pleated together, stapled in the center, and joined at the tips to form a Fourth of July decoration.

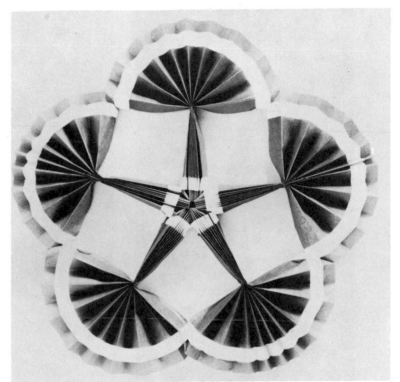

The same chain is pulled into a circle so that the inner pleats form a decorative star.

Pleat a piece of tissue paper, staple in the center, and cut out the shaded areas. Open into a snowflake and glue the sides.

Dainty snowflake cutouts, stapled in the center, form Christmas stars.

Snowflake pleats glued to form a chain.

Snowflake chain, this time pulled to a circle with the ends meeting in the center.

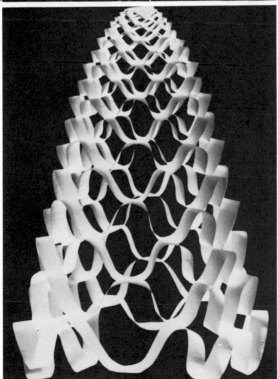

Fold a piece of tissue paper into sixteenths, and make cuts along the lines indicated.

Unfold and lift from the center. For the shape to hang freely it may be necessary to remove creases by pressing with a warm iron. Cutting alone changes a flat piece of tissue paper into this three-dimensional form.

Garlands and Honeycomb Decorations

The origin of garland-making is obscure, but the technique is particularly ingenious. By glueing cut pieces of tissue paper on alternate corners, a small quantity of paper can be turned into a chain many feet in length. If instead the adhesive is applied in parallel lines, the figure opens not in a chain but into a honeycomb, a different but equally intriguing effect.

In making either garlands or honeycomb designs, the proper adhesive is important. Ordinary white glue is suitable if used very sparingly and not allowed to penetrate more than one layer. A fast-drying clear cement—preferably from a tube with a small nozzle so that a fine line can be applied—is even better. Rubber cement, which remains sticky and tends to seep through several layers, should be avoided.

A number of methods can be used for making garlands. Once the principle is understood, the variety of chains that can be produced is virtually endless. Window displays, store decorations, and shops selling party supplies can all offer inspiration for new variations.

Garlands can be draped horizontally, hung vertically down a wall, stretched along the length of a party table, or shaped in rings and hung by ribbons from the ceiling. If a garland is particularly heavy and does not hang well, a long string can be passed through the center for added support. To make a framework for hanging rings, shape a length of wire into a circle and pass the ends through a garland chain before securing. Attach ribbons at three or four points along the ring for hanging.

Honeycomb decorations made by hand have a much fresher appearance than the traditional wedding bells and valentine hearts sold commercially. It is possible, of course, to imitate store-bought decorations, but with imagination many more original designs can be created. Colors, for example, can be combined to produce particularly interesting effects. The pear in the fruit bowl illustrated is much more vibrant for having been made from several colors of green and yellow-green. A honeycomb ball incorporating all the colors of the spectrum (yellow to red, blue, green, and then back to yellow again) makes a striking decoration. Madras tissue is also useful for producing a multicolored effect.

A GARLAND FROM EXPANDING CIRCLES

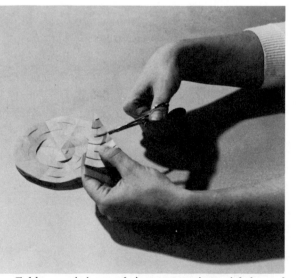

Fold several sheets of tissue paper into eighths and make cuts in from the fold along either side.

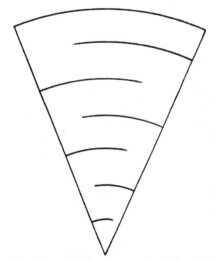

A pattern for cutting paper folded in eighths.

Glue the first two layers together at four points along the outer edge, then glue the next layer at the center only. Continue alternating between edges and center until a chain of the desired length is formed.

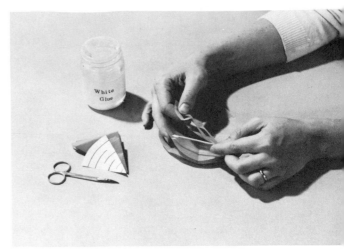

The completed garland in two shades of bright pink. Though only two sheets of 20- by 30-inch tissue paper were used, the chain is many feet in length.

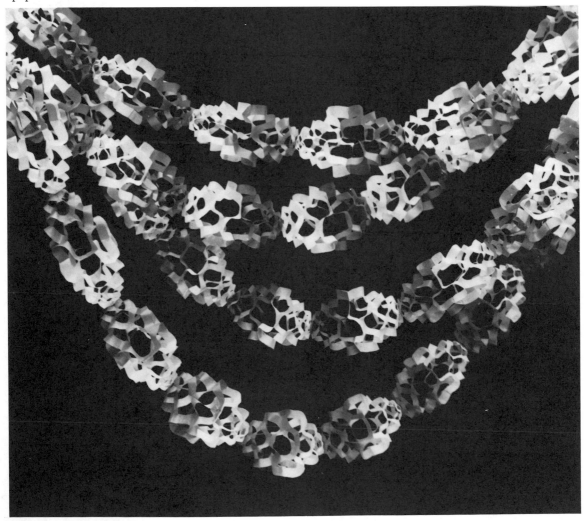

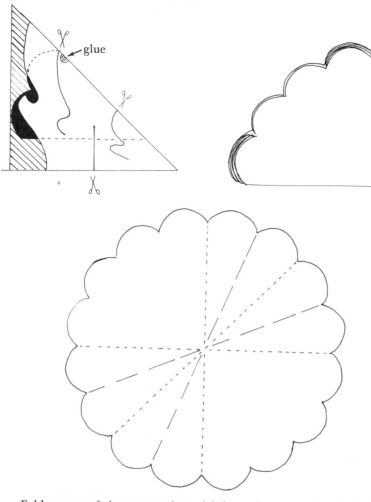

Fold squares of tissue paper into eighths, and cut away the shaded portion indicated in diagram (a). Make cuts indicated by scissors. Unfold and make a chain by glueing alternate layers at the corners and at the center. Cut flower shape (b) and make mountain and valley folds on the dotted lines to reach diagram (c). Insert two of these flowers between each double layer of the chain. The dotted line in figure (a) shows where the folded flower will lie and where it should be glued.

The finished garland is made of a green latticework chain punctuated by pink and yellow flowers.

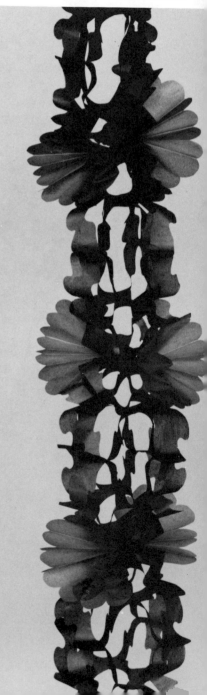

GARLANDS FROM CREASED SQUARES

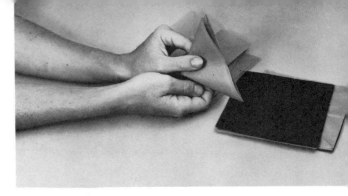

Many varieties of garlands can be made by this simple method. First, fold tissue squares into eighths to establish creases.

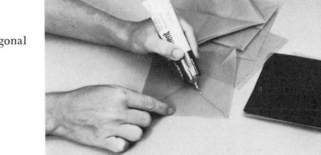

Apply fast-drying clear cement along the diagonal creases.

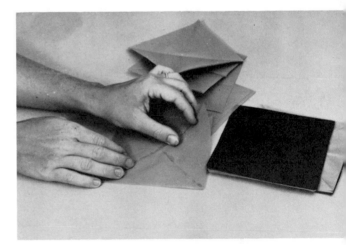

Lay a second piece of creased tissue paper on top.

This time apply adhesive to the horizontal and vertical creases. Continue until 12 to 18 sheets are glued in this manner.

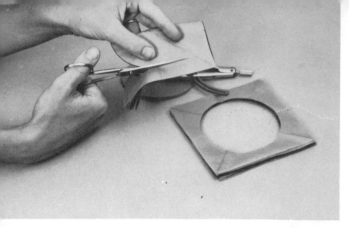

Cut out an area from the center. A number of stacks cut in the same manner can be joined for a long chain.

Three shapes cut from a single stack of glued tissue squares. The smallest circle was cut with scalloping shears.

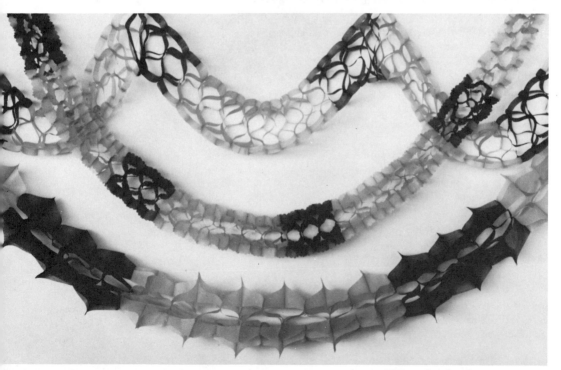

The garlands when expanded.

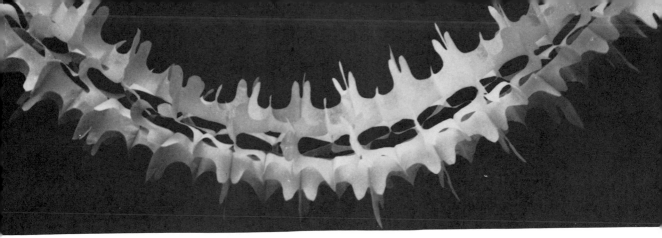

A multicolored garland cut in the same manner.

Pattern for a flower petal garland. Cut flowers and leaves from the same pattern. Glue all flower petals together at the tips and insert a leaf, glued at the center only, between each flower.

A flower petal garland with bright pink flowers and green leaves.

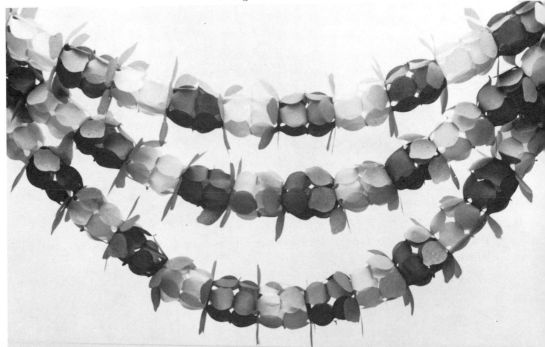

166

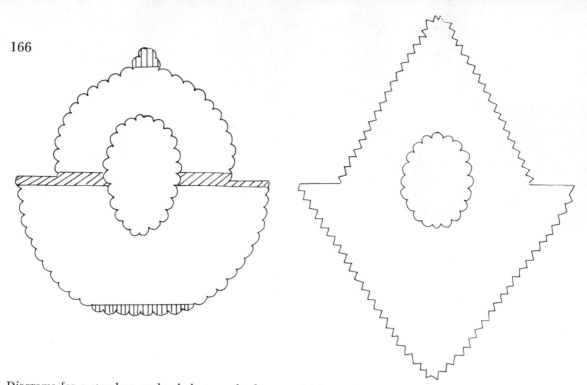

Diagrams for a stand-up garland that can be hung or laid on a flat surface. The shaded areas in the left figure show how glue is applied: first to the vertically lined area, then on alternate layers to the area shaded with diagonal lines.

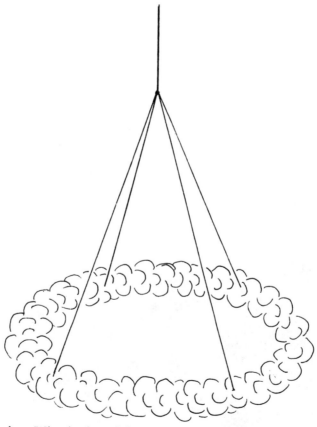

Diagram of a garland ring. Wire is shaped into a circle and ribbons attached at four points for hanging.

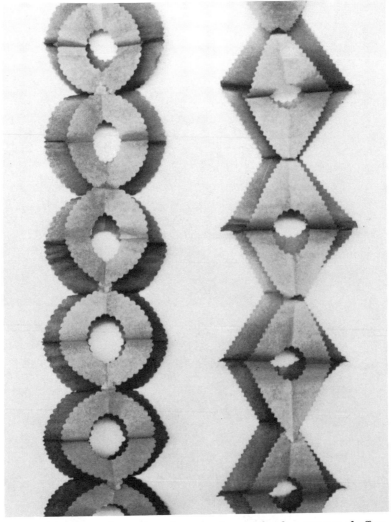

Striped or madras tissue gives these stand-up garlands a two-toned effect.

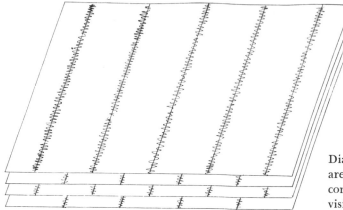

Diagram showing how alternate layers are glued for a honeycomb effect. Accordian pleat the paper to establish easily visible lines for glueing.

Glue even layers along the valley folds, odd layers along the mountain folds.

Glue cardboard to the front and back of the honeycomb shape, and reinforce top and bottom with paper tabs. Use small hairpins or other clips to hold the figures open.

A bowl of honeycomb fruit.

Cutting paper flowers from a stack of honeycomb tissue. Reinforce front and back with cardboard, then glue along the center seam and secure with paper tabs.

A delicate honeycomb flower in shades of light and dark pink.

Mobiles and Other Decorations

Often one decorative technique can be the inspiration for a number of designs. Porcupine balls are a case in point. Originating in Poland, these colorful balls were traditionally used to decorate the Christmas tree. They can also, however, be strung in a mobile, or cut in graduated sizes and assembled into a Christmas tree or an abstract re-creation of a dahlialike flower.

The technique used for the hanging decoration on page 172 could easily be elaborated in the same way. Three balls could, for instance, be stacked to make the body of a snowman, with features and a hat cut from construction paper. Or a square pattern could be substituted for the circular one and the resulting "petals" assembled into a colorful paper flower.

MOBILES

Mobiles are always effective decorations, and they are easy to make if a few simple rules are remembered. First, always start from the bottom when constructing a mobile. Hang two of the parts to be included from a support such as a bamboo skewer or a length of wire. Then determine the balancing point by resting the support on a ruler edge or other such object. Tie a knot at the point where the construction balances perfectly, and hang the balanced segment from the end of a second wooden or metal support. Continue adding parts until the mobile reaches the desired dimensions. Once fully assembled, the mobile can usually be adjusted by shifting the knots slightly (again, working from the bottom up). As a final step, secure the knots with a spot of glue so that a jolt will not throw the parts out of alignment. Hang wherever there is enough of a breeze to keep the mobile in motion.

To assemble a porcupine ball, pass a thread through the center of the shapes and also through a small round piece of cardboard (to prevent tearing). Tie the thread ends firmly and the pointed ends will spread naturally into a ball.

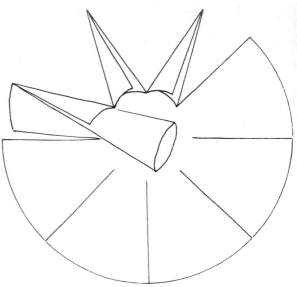

PORCUPINE BALLS

Pattern pieces for porcupine balls, a decoration of Polish origin.

Wrap each of the eight flaps over the tip of a paper cone and secure with thinned white glue applied with a brush. It helps to cover the cone with clear adhesive plastic so that the tissue paper does not stick.

A striking mobile in brilliant yellow, red, and orange.

CHRISTMAS TREE

Use graduated shapes in several colors of green tissue paper to make a Christmas tree. Gummed reinforcements strengthen the centers, which are slipped over a dowel inserted in a Styrofoam base.

For ornaments, glue silver candies to the tips of the branches. Top the tree with a silver ball.

Tiny tissue-wrapped packages shaped from Styrofoam and tied with gold thread lie in wait under the decorated tree.

"Dahlias" are made from the same pattern. Use a smaller size star for the center. Cut an eight-pointed star from cardboard to reinforce the back set of petals.

HANGING MOBILE

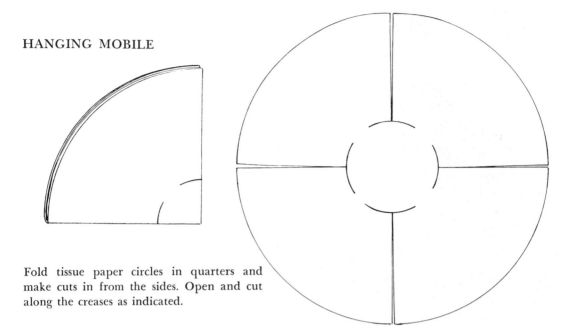

Fold tissue paper circles in quarters and make cuts in from the sides. Open and cut along the creases as indicated.

Glue each of the sides over a paper cone. String about twenty of the shapes together and tie as for the porcupine balls.

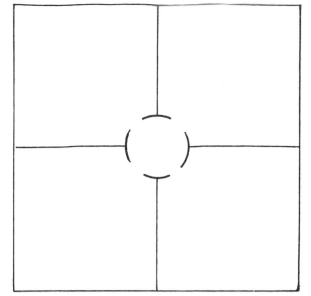

The same method can be used with a square piece of paper to make a fanciful flower.

Fold tissue paper circles into quarters without creasing. String a thread through the tip of each folded shape and tie firmly. Fluff the shape into a ball.

Folded circles make a Christmas ball.

Hanging mobile in graduated sizes.

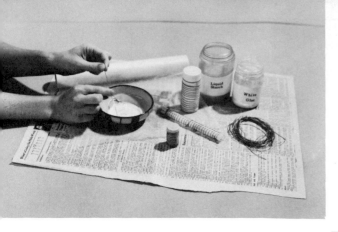

GOLD FILIGREE BALLS

Soak gold cord in a mixture of white glue and liquid starch, then wrap around assorted round objects that have been covered with wax paper.

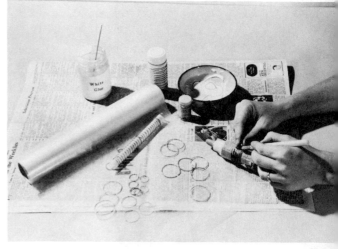

When thoroughly dry, cut the shapes off the molds and remove. Use thick white glue to join the tips of each of the resulting circles.

Dip the circles lightly in thinned white glue, then lay on the surface of a balloon. Cover one half of the balloon at a time, using extra white glue to secure each joint. Continue covering the whole balloon but leave a line around the middle where the joints are not glued so that the design can be separated into two halves.

When thoroughly dry, deflate the balloon and glue tissue circles to the inside of the shell. Rejoin the two halves and hang.

Gold filigree balls from tissue paper and gold cord.

11

DESIGNS FROM TWO-SIDED PAPER

Often a tool or material that has great usefulness in one profession is ignored or unknown in others. Dry mounting tissue, most often used by photographers for fastening photographs without glue, is such a product. When used to fuse two layers of tissue, it creates a new and unexpected material: an opaque two-color paper, heavier than construction paper, and very different from tissue paper in its basic properties.

Most dry mounting tissues require a dry mounting press with high heat to melt the adhesive that serves to bond the surfaces. One kind, however, has a waxy surface with a low melting point suitable for application with an iron.* It comes in sheets or rolls, and is available at most large photographic stores. Unlike other dry mounting papers, which tend to have a yellowish tint, the waxy type has a white surface that does not discolor the tissue paper, but renders it opaque so that the front and back layers appear as two distinct colors.

Start by placing a sheet of dry mounting tissue between two sheets of tissue paper. Since there is a tendency for large surfaces to wrinkle, it is best to trim the dry mounting tissue and the tissue paper to a man-

* Fotoflat, a waxy white dry mounting tissue, is manufactured by the Seal Company of Derby, Connecticut.

ageable size, slightly larger than the design to be cut out.

Next, sandwich these layers between two sheets of newsprint to protect the surfaces from excess wax that may leak out. Let the iron heat to a temperature between low and medium (do not, of course, use steam, as the moisture would spot the tissue paper). Hold the iron over one section for about five to ten seconds—do not move it back and forth—then lift and rub the heated area with a cloth or crumpled paper towel. Since the dry mounting tissue adheres as it cools, this rubbing is an important step. Move the iron to a new section and repeat the heating and rubbing until the whole area is joined. It is possible to speed the process by moving the iron onto a new section to heat while the previously heated segment is being rubbed with a cloth.

Any areas that become smudged or where the wax has penetrated the tissue paper can be cleaned with a solvent such as rubber cement thinner or lighter fluid.

The finished material can be cut, scored, folded, or curled like any other paper of similar weight. It is most effective when shaped into simple geometric designs that rely on line and shape rather than excessive decoration for their impact. Variations in color provided by the two-toned effect will accent the shape of three-dimensional figures and provide all the decorative interest necessary.

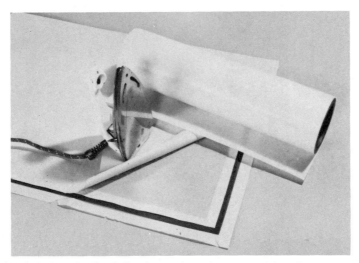

Stack papers in the following order: clean newsprint (for protection), tissue paper, waxy dry mounting paper, tissue paper of a contrasting color, newsprint. Press briefly with a warm iron, then rub with a crumpled cloth.

180

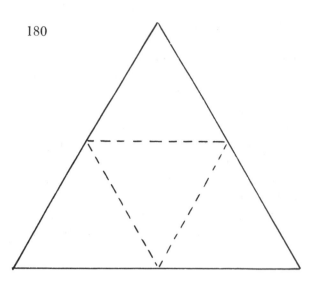

CONSTRUCTIONS FROM A TRIANGLE

Fold upward on the dotted lines and curl the three corners by drawing over a scissor blade. Glue the three tips together.

Glue the shapes in various combinations for a mobile or Christmas decorations.

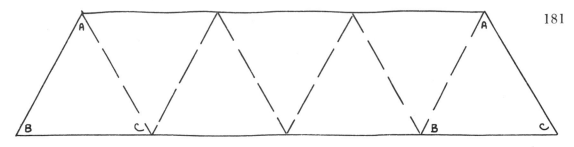

OPEN-SIDED OCTAHEDRONS

Mountain fold on all the dotted lines, and glue the first flap over the last so that points A, B, and C meet.

Octahedrons in assorted sizes. The inside color differs from that on the outside.

Flowers made from circles of laminated paper are cut to the center, then curled over a scissor blade.

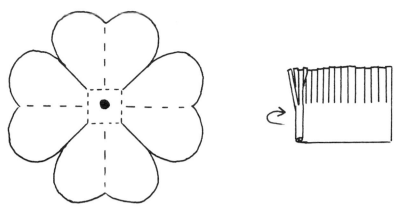

FLOWER TREE

Cut flowers as indicated and fold on the dotted lines. Insert a fringed flower center cut from two-sided paper.

Flower centers are inserted in holes stuck in a Styrofoam ball to form a flower tree.

INCISED TRIANGLE

Different colors predominate as the ornament turns, showing its different faces.

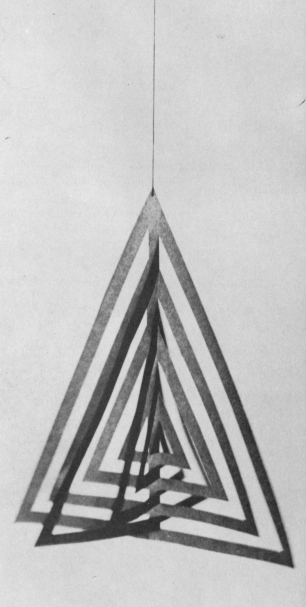

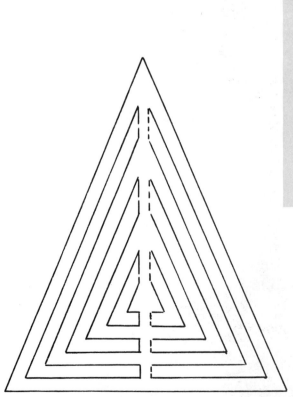

Cut on the solid lines and fold on the dotted lines, bringing alternate strips on the right side forward, and folding the equivalent strips on the left side to the back.

HANGING INCISED CIRCLE

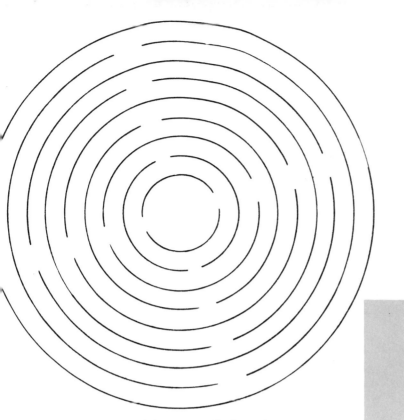

Cut on all the solid lines, then lift from the center.

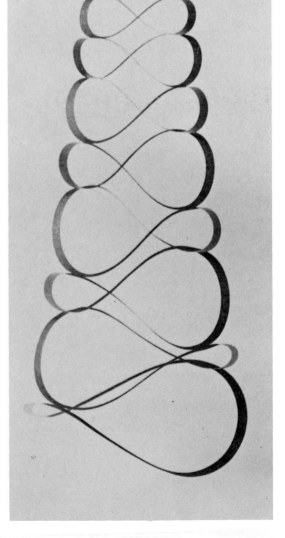

Graceful symmetry characterizes this blue and green design.

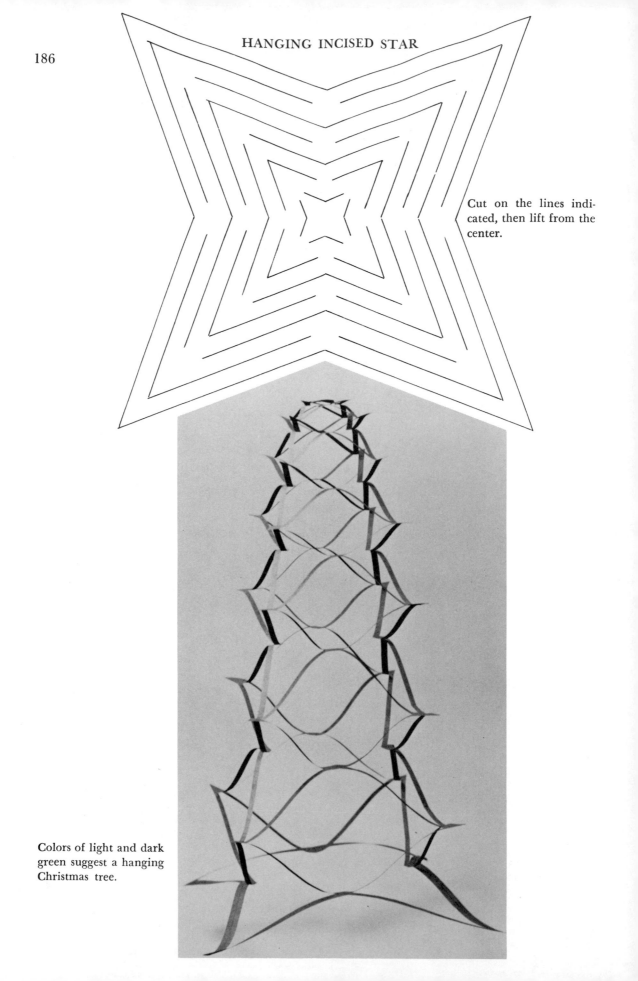

HANGING INCISED STAR

Cut on the lines indicated, then lift from the center.

Colors of light and dark green suggest a hanging Christmas tree.

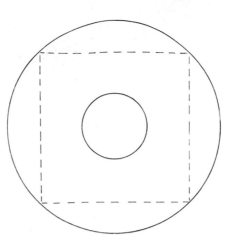

GEOMETRICAL CONSTRUCTIONS

Cut out the figures and fold upward on the dotted lines.

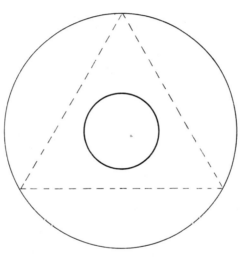

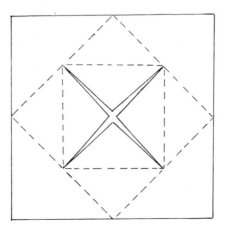

Colorful geometric constructions based on: (a) a square inscribed in a circle, (b) a triangle in a circle, and (c) a square within a square.

STAR-SHAPED ORNAMENTS

Take a strip of double-sided paper twice as long as it is wide. Fold and crease as indicated so that the upper left- and right-hand corners meet.

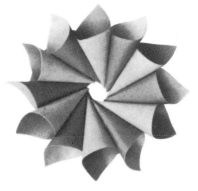

Combine these shapes in a number of ways to form starlike patterns.

Take three or more strips of double-sided paper, each slightly longer than the next, and fold in thirds, fourths, or fifths. Glue strips together at each fold.

Arrange the resulting strips in curved or starlike formations.

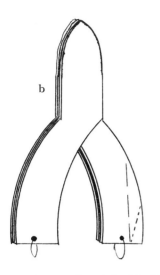

b

COLLAPSIBLE FOLDING ORNAMENT

a

Cut a long strip of double-sided paper as shown in diagram (a). Valley and mountain fold on the dotted lines to reach diagram (b). Fasten a wire through the bottom of each side, then open out the figure as it is or crease each flap as indicated by the dotted lines to reveal more of the color underneath.

The figure fully opened. The colors are reversed on the opposite side.

12

LAMPSHADES

Lampshades made from tissue paper are both attractive and functional. The soft folds of the tissue paper filter the harsh glare of electric light and produce a glow that is warm and pleasing. The use of natural materials and simple frameworks creates a look both rustic and sophisticated. Although fragile in appearance, lampshades from tissue paper are surprisingly durable; they can be counted on to withstand years of use.

Naturally, since paper will burn, certain precautions are necessary when choosing to make lampshades of this material. A few of the smaller shades described in this chapter are intended as room accents; they should be used with bulbs no stronger than 15 or 25 watts. Larger shades, however, can accommodate greater wattage: the 16-inch papier-mâché lampshade shown here has been in use for over two years with a 200-watt bulb.

If desired, chemicals are available that can be dissolved in the glue mixture used with tissue paper lampshades to reduce their flammability. City fire departments are always willing to help with the selection of fireproofing materials; do not hesitate to consult them. More important is common sense in the use of electrical

Soft light radiates from a papier-mâché lampshade molded around a 16-inch beach ball. The finished lamp is large enough to accommodate a 200-watt bulb.

wiring. Choose only materials tested and approved by Underwriters Laboratories (bearing the UL label) and, if you have never wired a lamp before, get advice from an electrical supply store or from a licensed electrician.

Papier-Mâché Lampshades

Given the simple beauty of these lamps, it is surprising how easy they are to make. Strips of torn tissue paper are wrapped around a mold, coated with a glue and water mixture, and allowed to dry. When the mold is removed and a bulb inserted, the light radiates through the folds in a soft glow.

Most any object can be chosen as a mold for papier-mâché lampshades provided it can be easily removed once the tissue paper is dry. Inflatable objects, such as balloons or beach balls, are ideal. Plastic bowls are also suitable, especially if the lampshade is to be made in two parts and then joined when the mold is removed. Any object that might stick to the tissue paper—metal or wood, for example—can be covered with kitchen plastic wrap. When dry the tissue paper and plastic wrap are gently pulled off the mold, and the plastic torn away and discarded.

White glue is the essential ingredient that stiffens the tissue paper and enables it to hold its shape. It is thinned half-and-half with water, then brushed either on the mold or on the tissue paper itself. A large lampshade may require several cups of the mixture; therefore it is much more economical to purchase glue in quart or half-gallon containers.

Either white or colored tissue paper may be used to make papier-mâché lampshades. White is especially attractive, but colored tissue may be pleasing when a decorative effect is desired. The two require slightly different techniques for application.

If using white tissue paper, choose the inexpensive variety usually sold in packets as wrapping or packing tissue. This is softer than dyed tissue paper, and easier to apply. Tear it in thirds or fourths lengthwise—a torn edge is easier to conceal than a cut one.

Next choose and prepare a mold. A peach ball can be used as it is; a balloon can be given a light coating of Vaseline or salad oil. (Though not a necessary step, this helps if the balloon should burst before the tissue is fully dry.) Metal or wooden objects should be covered with plastic wrap.

Using a paintbrush, apply the glue and water mixture directly to the surface of the mold. Lightly crush the tissue paper, then wrap the first strip, overlapping slightly with each turn. When one or two strips are applied, paint the surface with more of the glue mixture. Continue until the mold is covered, allowing an opening large enough for the light fixture to pass.

Place the completed form in a warm place to dry. If using a balloon as a mold, make sure the spot is not too warm, or the balloon may expand and burst. Do not try to loosen the mold until the tissue paper is completely dry or the tissue is likely to collapse. When fully dry, the mold should pull away easily from the sides of the tissue paper shell.

Colored tissue paper is less fragile than white wrapping tissue, so the glue can be applied directly to the paper before wrapping it around the mold. Once it is wrapped, recoat the outer surface only if there remain unsecured areas—colored tissue paper is less absorbent than wrapping tissue, and the glue may remain on the surface to give an unpleasant shiny appearance when dry.

When completed, lampshades made by the papier-mâché method can be hung from the ceiling or used as table or floor lamps. Smaller versions make colorful Christmas decorations when strung with miniature Christmas lights. If a hole is allowed in both top and bottom, round or elongated shapes can also serve as softly glowing candle holders.

Torn strips of tissue paper and thinned white glue are the basic materials needed. Beach balls, balloons, or plastic containers make good molds. Vaseline or plastic wrap are used on the mold only if there is a likelihood the tissue paper will stick.

Paint thinned white glue liberally on the balloon's surface. Steady the balloon in a bowl.

Begin wrapping with strips of tissue paper, overlapping slightly with each turn.

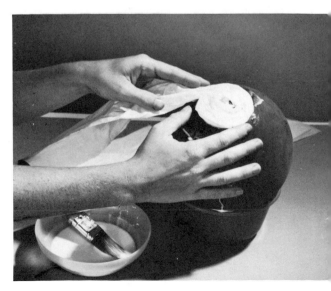

Coat the surface of the tissue paper once more with glue. Continue wrapping and glueing until the balloon is covered except for an opening at the top. For a candle holder leave openings at both top and bottom.

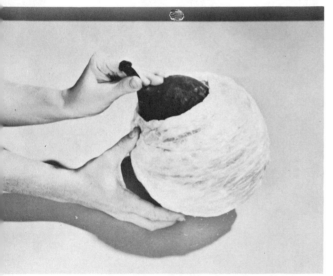

When the tissue paper is completely dry, deflate the balloon. It will pull away from the sides easily.

Colored tissue paper is treated differently: thinned white glue is brushed directly on the tissue paper before it is wound around the mold.

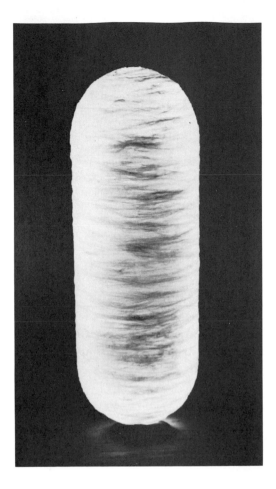

A metal wastebasket covered with newspaper (to allow the mold to slip out easily) and plastic wrap (to prevent sticking) provides the basic mold for this cylindrical lampshade. Balloons inserted in each end of the dried tissue paper cylinder are used to make the rounded ends. White Christmas tree lights provide the illumination, avoiding "hot spots" that might be produced by a single strong bulb.

Tiny Christmas tree bulbs light these gaily colored Christmas balls.

Parchment Lampshades

When two sheets of tissue paper are laminated together using white glue, the result is a parchmentlike material. If applied to a framework while still damp, it will shrink on drying to produce sculptured curves. If allowed to dry first, the parchment can be shaped into a variety of flat-surfaced geometrical designs.

MAKING TISSUE PAPER PARCHMENT

To fuse two sheets of tissue paper into one, thinned white glue is used. Since soft wrapping tissue tends to tear when damp, use instead the stiffer, sized variety sold by the manufacturers of colored tissue paper. First lay a sheet of white tissue paper on a nonabsorbent surface such as a kitchen counter top. Then brush liberally with a mixture of white glue diluted half and half with water. Immediately cover with a second sheet of tissue paper, laying it on smoothly to avoid large wrinkles. Cover this in turn with a sheet of clear kitchen plastic wrap and roll the whole surface with a rubber roller. Ignore the small wrinkles produced by rolling; they add a decorative effect when dry.

Next, remove the plastic wrap and carefully pick up the damp tissue paper. Hang to dry from a towel rack or clothesline—the glue may hold it in place, or clothespins may be necessary. Make sure the damp tissue does not come in contact with any other surface while drying, or its shape may become distorted.

Lay tissue paper on a nonabsorbent surface and brush with thinned white glue.

Cover with a second piece of tissue paper, then with clear plastic wrap. Use the roller to press out any air bubbles. Remove the plastic wrap and hang to dry.

Damp parchment glued to a frame will have a sculptured effect when dry. Cover one segment at a time, allow to dry, and trim off any excess.

LAMPSHADES FROM DAMP PARCHMENT

If using the parchment damp, let it dry long enough to become manageable (it will still be sticky but will not tear as easily as when wet). Coat the framework to be covered with white glue (preferably the thicker "tacky" white glue sold in hobby shops) and lay on a piece of damp parchment cut slightly larger than the area to be covered. Allow the segment to dry, then trim off any overlapping areas. A hair dryer blowing warm air can be used to speed the drying.

Frameworks for sculptured lampshades can be of wood, metal, or any other material desired. Metal should be of a nonrusting kind, or it will discolor due to the effects of the water-based glue. The framework for the hanging lamp shown above was made by securing thin wooden dowels through holes drilled in embroidery rings. For the table lamp illustrated, six lengths of piano wire were joined in the center with epoxy cement, with the ends radiating outward to make twelve spokes. These twelve wires were then pulled downward and inserted in holes punched in a ring cut from a stiff cardboard tube. The ends were secured to the cardboard tube with epoxy, and the framework covered. Finally, the base of the lampshade was inserted in a bamboo drinking cup and wired to accommodate a 25-watt bulb.

Wooden dowels are inserted in holes drilled diagonally through wooden embroidery rings to make a framework for a lampshade of sculptured parchment paper.

A bamboo drinking cup makes a handsome base for a lampshade constructed with piano wire. A long narrow bulb was chosen to fit through the lampshade's narrow opening.

LAMPSHADES FROM DRY PARCHMENT

The easiest lampshades to make from dry parchment are those based on geometrical solids such as the cube, icosahedron, or dodecahedron. Folding lamps are also striking. For inspiration, skim through a textbook on geometry or one on mathematical models. (Suggested sources are listed in the Bibliography at the back of the book.)

The basic technique is simple. Dried parchment is laid flat, supports are glued on, and the excess paper trimmed away. The figure is then drawn up and glued into its finished shape, with an opening left to accommodate a light fixture. If a single piece of parchment is inadequate, joins can be made along any seam covered by a support; they will be virtually invisible when the lampshade is assembled.

Wooden dowels, bamboo skewers (or matchstick bamboo taken from place mats or blinds), and medical applicator sticks * are some of the materials most useful for making a framework. Cut them to the proper size and fasten to the parchment

* Generally of a standard 6-inch length, medical applicator sticks can be ordered in boxes of 100 or more from pharmacies or medical supply houses. They were used in the icosahedron lampshade shown on page 201, and were cut to 3-inch lengths for the star lampshade on page 203.

with white glue. At places where a number of supports meet, allow about 1/8 to 1/4 inch free space so that the parchment will not tear when folded into its finished shape. If a pattern is necessary, draw it in dark ink on white paper and insert it under the translucent parchment; the lines will show through as guides for placing the supports.

The star lantern on page 211 is less complicated than it looks; it is based on a simple icosahedron. Instead of flat planes, however, twenty pyramid shapes are constructed and glued at their bases, one pyramid occupying each triangle of the icosahedron diagram. One of the pyramids is left unglued on two sides of its base so that the shape can be opened to admit a small light.

Parchment lampshades are somewhat fragile, but since they are generally hung in undisturbed locations, they can be counted on to last a long time. Also, they are remarkably easy to repair: should a tear develop, simply cut out the damaged section and replace it with a fresh piece of parchment cut to size.

White glue is used to fasten wooden sticks to dry parchment paper. Flaps are allowed for glueing the assembled shape. One triangle is left unglued so that it can swing back to allow a light fixture to enter.

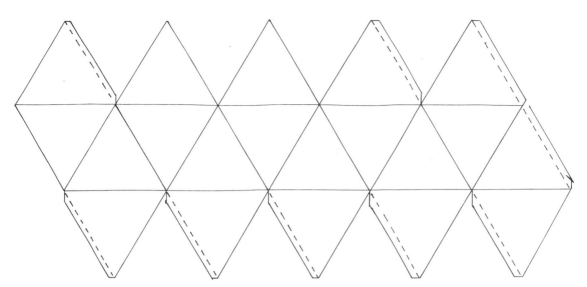

Pattern for an icosahedron lampshade. The solid lines indicate wooden dowels; the dotted lines are flaps for glueing. One flap is left unglued on two sides.

An icosahedron lampshade from dry parchment paper.

A parchment lampshade based on a dodecahedron, a solid
with twelve faces of five sides each. The design of wooden
skewers inside each five-sided plane is purely decorative.

Pattern for a dodecahedron lampshade. Glue a support to every other side around the exterior of the
diagram. Allow flaps for glueing on the remaining sides. Make a hole for inserting a light in the middle
of one of the pentagons.

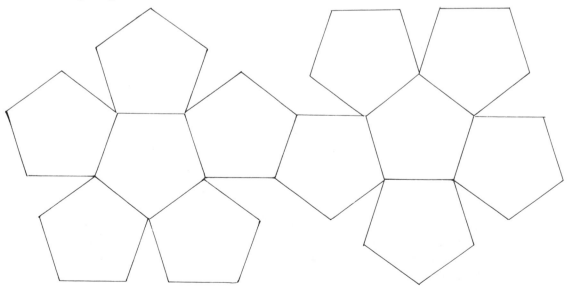

A star-shaped lampshade with twenty points makes a decorative Christmas hanging.

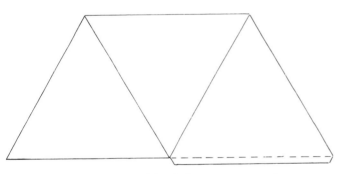

Make twenty pyramids of tissue paper parchment. Place one on each of the triangles in the icosahedron diagram previously shown, and glue where the bases meet. Then draw the ends together and glue the remaining sides to form a star.

Several sheets of tissue paper parchment are needed for this lampshade. It is creased in such a way as to make it collapsible for storage.

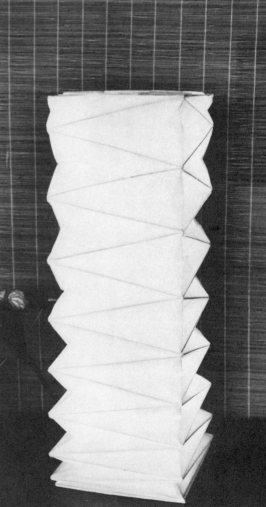

Lampshades with Flowers and Leaves

Lampshades incorporating plant materials have a fresh and natural appearance. The tissue paper that covers the plants seals and protects them without obscuring their natural beauty. Almost any kind of flower or leaf (provided it is not too large or bulky) can be used. The plants should be prepared in the usual manner, by pressing under newspaper or between pages of a book until most of the moisture is removed. Some plant colors are unstable and will tend to fade even after being sealed under tissue paper, but their beauty when silhouetted by the light will remain unchanged.

Medium or heavy-weight acetate provides the base to which the tissue paper can adhere. This is coated with a mixture of white glue and water and the plant materials laid in place. A sheet of white tissue paper is laid on top, covered with a piece of plastic wrap, and rollered to remove air bubbles. The plastic wrap is removed and the layers allowed to dry, after which a second sheet of tissue paper is glued to the underside of the acetate. The two sheets of tissue paper serve to diffuse the electric light and to conceal all traces of the acetate.

Once the sheets containing the plant materials are prepared, they can be fastened to a flat surface or curved to a cylindrical shape. They can also be fastened to a shoji-type window framework to provide privacy while still allowing ample light to pass.

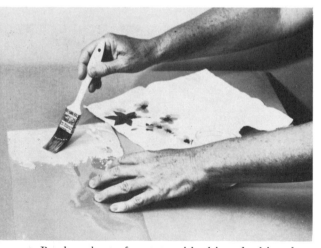

Brush a sheet of acetate with thinned white glue.

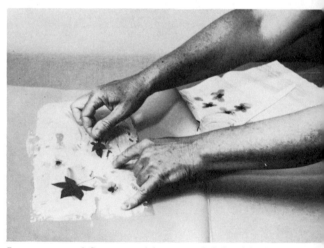

Lay on pressed flowers and leaves and dab with the glue mixture.

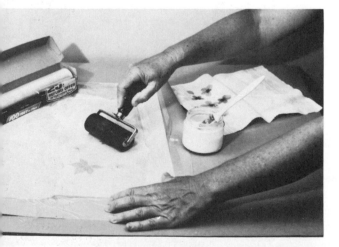

Cover with tissue paper, then with plastic wrap, and roll to remove any air bubbles. When dry, reverse and glue a second sheet of tissue paper to the back of the acetate.

Notched wood makes the framework for a rectangular lamp. The leaves are sealed between tissue paper and acetate.

Embroidery rings and wooden dowels, rounded at one end, support a cylindrical lampshade decorated with colorful autumn leaves. Use only small leaves; large ones cause the acetate to buckle.

Yellow flowers and green leaves decorate a candle holder secured at the top and bottom with cane handbag handles. The flowers have kept their colors for over two years.

Shoji-type window covering with tissue paper and acetate panels. This treatment offers privacy while still allowing light to pass.

A close-up showing how light passing through a plant silhouettes the flowers and accentuates the leaf veins.

Other Lampshade Techniques

Tissue paper does not necessarily have to be treated to be used in a lampshade. Although less durable, lampshades using ordinary tissue paper can be used as colorful sources of light and decoration.

The circus lamp shown below is an example. Animal silhouettes are cut from black wrapping paper that has a white backing. They are laid dark side down on a sheet of firm white paper, and covered with a colorful piece of tissue paper. A shiny-surfaced paper in which slits have been cut covers the other layers and serves as the zoo bars. When the lamp is turned off, the animals are invisible; they make their appearance only when the light is lit.

The other photograph shows but one of a whole range of lampshades that can be made by cutting openings in stiff paper and covering these with tissue paper. The shade illustrated is cut from bright red paper with a velvet finish; yellow-orange tissue is glued inside. It emits a warm, orange-colored light that is highly decorative.

Cast-off materials can often be used for imaginative lampshades. Here a screw-top can is spray painted, wired, and topped with a paper shade fastened to a large embroidery ring. The circus animals disappear when the light is off.

Materials used in making the circus lamp.

Colored tissue paper backs the cutout design areas of this icosahedron lampshade.

Star shades also make impressive seasonal decorations. Pyramid star points are glued to an icosahedron cut from two-ply bristol board. Holes are cut in the icosahedron and covered with tissue paper. Since the light is filtered through two layers of tissue paper, the resulting effect is diffuse and glowing.

Pattern for an icosahedron-based star lampshade. Cut from two-ply or heavier paper.

Cut out the circles and cover the shape with tissue paper to filter the light.

Fold and cut dark-colored tissue paper, and glue to a second sheet of lighter color tissue.

Glue on wooden dowels and shape to form a pyramid. Twenty such pyramids are needed for a star.

The light glows like stained glass through the cutout design.

A simpler version in three shades of green.

13

LIGHT AND SHADE

Using light with tissue paper opens whole new design possibilities. When tissue is folded and lit from behind, the pattern of the folds and the deepening intensity of the color are clearly apparent. When different colors are overlapped, new colors emerge, red and yellow combining to make orange, blue and yellow to produce green. Starting with the approximately forty basic colors of commercially dyed tissue, the possible color combinations are almost endless.

This chapter presents some of the techniques that take advantage of the transparent quality of tissue paper. Some make use of tissue paper alone, others combine materials such as wax or plastic to change the quality of light as it passes through the paper.

Experimenting with Tissue Paper and Light

Different effects can be produced by folding tissue paper into flat or three-dimensional shapes. Hold flat figures such as the origami designs illustrated to the light and the folds stand out in a striking pattern. In another photograph three-dimen-

213

sional shapes are used instead of flat designs—their beauty lies not only in the pattern of the folds but also in the subtle modeling of color from light to dark.

Stencil effects can be achieved by cutting shapes from opaque paper and filling the empty spaces with tissue. The colors glow like stained glass when held to the light. A new dimension is added by overlapping different colors as shown. Here cutouts of gold paper faced with tissue are combined to produce multicolored patterns.

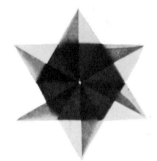

Origami folds held to the light produce a striking design.

Subtle modulation from light to dark characterizes these three-dimensional folded stars.

Light passing through cutout stencils is colored by the tissue paper that fills the spaces.

Gold paper medallions. Overlapping two or more shapes
produces new and interesting
color combinations.

Colorful designs cut from folded tissue paper are sandwiched between wax-impregnated layers.

Place tissue paper on a piece of cardboard and melt paraffin wax onto it. Alternate layers of cutout designs and plain tissue paper.

Wax Medallions

Wax can be used instead of glue to combine layers of tissue paper to produce intriguing patterns. An iron is used to melt paraffin wax onto white or colored tissue paper and a cutout design laid flat on top. More layers are added and the whole pressed with an iron to spread the wax and fuse the paper. Hang the resulting medallion against the window and the different layers and overlapping patterns will be illuminated.

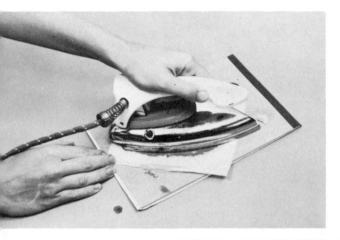

Spread the wax and fuse the layers by pressing with a warm iron. Peel the layers from the cardboard while still warm, then trim to size.

Wax medallions using colored tissue paper can be overlapped for interesting color effects.

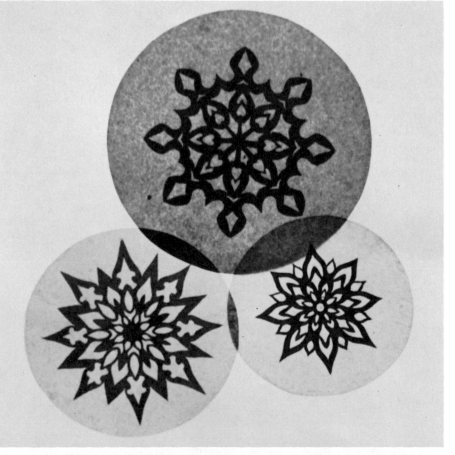

Shadow Puppets

Shadow puppetry is an ancient art of great charm. Most traditional shadow puppets are made either of an opaque material, which appears as a black silhouette, or of a translucent substance such as leather, which is painted for a colorful effect. Generally the figures are held close to a white screen and lit from behind, with the lighting directed in such a way that the rods manipulating the puppets are not seen.

Tissue paper provides a colorful substitute for the materials traditionally used in making shadow puppets. One method, a silhouette technique, is shown in the accompanying series of photographs. Here the puppets are cut from black paper, and the cutout areas filled with colored tissue. Tissue paper is also used for the scenery: four layers of a light-colored paper are piled one upon the next to give a feeling of distance from the light background to the darker foreground.

A second technique abandons the silhouette approach and relies instead on the color of the tissue paper to define the shapes of the figures. The body parts are cut from sheets of stiff acetate and then decorated with tissue paper held in place with spray cement. A black oil-base felt pen (water-base inks will not adhere to acetate) can be used to outline the puppet's

A STORY TOLD WITH SHADOW PUPPETS:
The Wedding of the Swordfish

The Swordfish comes in search of the King to marry him to his Seahorse Sweetheart. When asked where the King is, the Fish respond that he's sleeping, as usual.

But the Swordfish spots the King's crown, and he plunges as the Fish look on in alarm.

Out comes the startled King, rudely awakened from his deep sleep to find himself . . .

. . . in an awkward position. He calls for help, promising to grant a wish to the one who comes to his aid.

The Swordfish, winking at his friends, offers his "humble services" to the King, and seats him properly.

The King mumbles a drowsy "thank you," and is about to doze again when the Swordfish reminds him of his promise.

So the King pronounces Swordfish and Sweetheart Seahorse man and wife, then climbs happily back to bed as the Fish cheer . . .

. . . and begin a dance to celebrate the marriage of the happy couple.

features. The completed figures are covered with a sheet of clear adhesive-backed film to protect the surfaces from dirt and moisture.

Shadow puppets with moving parts can be joined with paper fasteners, wire, cotton or nylon thread, or any material that is not too bulky and will allow the parts to move freely. In the case of acetate puppets, transparent nylon thread (or fishing line) is the least conspicuous. Knot it on either side of the figure, and place a dab of glue on the knots so that they cannot work free.

Lighting is determined by the kind of rods used to manipulate the puppets. Shadow puppets on horizontal rods (i.e., at right angles to the figures) are illuminated by lights fixed just below and behind the screen. The rods cast no shadow on the staging area, and are therefore invisible. Puppets attached to perpendicular rods are lit from above and behind. The main support for the puppet is generally held below the screen and out of sight. Rods manipulating heads and arms, however, will cast a shadow, but if inconspicuous materials (such as thin wire or strips of rigid acetate) are used, their appearance will in no way detract from the puppets' appearance.

A third technique is designed not for a live audience but for the camera. Here the stage (preferably a sheet of glass) is placed in a horizontal position, and the lighting directed up from below. The puppets are placed on top of the glass and moved by hand between camera shots, thus eliminating the need for rods. This method is suitable either for still photography, or for imaginative animated films such as those produced by filmmaker Lotte Reiniger. (For her book on the subject, and for more detailed information on the construction of shadow puppets and the staging of puppet plays, consult the books on puppetry listed in the Bibliography.)

Materials for making a puppet from stiff acetate. Fasten the tissue to the acetate with spray cement, and cover the completed puppet with clear adhesive film.

Acetate-backed puppets. The boy doffs his hat, the girl holds up her flowers.

A juggling jester. Face and body parts are outlined in black ink.

Giant "stained glass" butterfly is made of polyester resin colored with red and yellow tissue paper. It has a wing spread of two feet.

Whimsical animals from colored tissue paper and polyester resin. The shapes are outlined with a glue and powdered poster color mixture.

Stained Glass

Tissue paper has the intriguing characteristic of becoming transparent when coated with substances such as lacquer, liquid acrylic, or liquid polyester resin. Lacquer or liquid acrylic can simply be painted on the tissue, producing a material resembling cellophane. Plastic resin, being more viscous, creates an effect closer to glass. When castings of tissue paper and polyester resin are held to the light, they have the same glowing brilliance characteristic of stained glass.

TISSUE PAPER AND LIQUID POLYESTER RESIN

Polyester resin comes as a syrupy liquid that hardens on the addition of a small amount of catalyst. The catalyst sets off a chain reaction known as polymerization, whereby the molecules of the liquid resin join to become a solid. The cure proceeds slowly in cool conditions, but is speeded by the addition of heat. Thin castings need extra catalyst to generate the heat required for polymerization, while thick castings require less. (Indeed, too much heat can cause a thick casting to fracture.)

For coloring polyester resin, tissue paper has certain advantages over resin dyes. It can be incorporated in the casting before the resin is poured or brushed on after the piece has catalyzed. In multicolored castings it is hard to keep resin dyes from spilling out of the chamber for which they are intended and mingling with a neighboring color. Tissue paper, by contrast, can be cut to the precise size of the area to be colored. Finally, tissue paper can be layered and colors combined to produce any intensity and hue desired.

WORKING WITH POLYESTER RESIN

Since resin is sticky and difficult to remove, use disposable tools whenever possible. Pour the uncatalyzed resin into paper cups, and stir in the catalyst with a wooden skewer or tongue depressor. Use nylon brushes for applying tissue paper (hardware stores carrying fiber glass supplies sell inexpensive ones) since they are easier to clean than brushes made of animal hair. Reusable tools can be cleaned before the resin has set by scrubbing in hot soapy water. Hardened resin requires the use of a strong solvent such as acetone or lacquer thinner for removal.

To prepare the resin for casting, pour the desired amount into a paper cup marked on the side in ounces. Following the manufacturer's directions, add the required number of drops of catalyst from a squeeze bottle, using more for a thin casting and less for a thick one. Since different brands may gel at different rates, some experimentation may be necessary. Stir until thoroughly mixed—i.e., until the hairlines formed by the catalyst in the resin have disappeared. In general, gentle stirring is desired to avoid air bubbles, but an interesting effect can be achieved by intentionally incorporating air with vigorous stirrings of a paintbrush.

Now pour the catalyzed resin into the prepared mold (molds are discussed below). Within a short amount of time—varying with the thickness of the casting and the amount of catalyst added—the resin will begin to gel. At this stage it will have a rubbery texture and can be trimmed with a knife or pointed instrument such as an awl or needle. Placing the casting in a warm place (such as a closed oven with the oven light turned on) will speed the curing time.*

Sometimes the surface of a casting exposed to the air will develop a sticky residue, especially if the piece has been undercatalyzed. Generally, surface tack can be eliminated by brushing on a coat of highly catalyzed resin. In some instances, however, the problem may be in the resin itself: polyester resin has a limited shelf life, and stale resin may never catalyze satisfactorily. Thus, it is important to purchase supplies only from stores that keep fresh material in stock.

If tissue paper is not incorporated in the casting before it is cured, it can be applied afterward using a paintbrush and heavily catalyzed resin. First cut tissue

* Thin castings can generally take even more heat. Some manufacturers advise allowing them to sit in a 200° oven for about 15 minutes. When removed, they will still feel tacky, but after they cool the surface should be tack free.

paper to the desired size. Brush resin on the area of the casting to be covered, lay the tissue paper in place, and coat again with resin. Build up layers and combine colors until the desired intensity is reached, then allow the resin to harden.

MOLDS

A number of different materials can be used as molds for making imitation stained glass. Glue, metal, and clay are some of the possibilities. All require the use of acetate or Mylar (a dense, flexible plastic similar to acetate) as a backing sheet. The acetate pulls away easily from the hardened resin, leaving a smooth, tack-free surface.

Glue

If ordinary white glue is mixed with powdered poster color, it forms a paste that can be extruded from a plastic squeeze bottle. When dry, the glue mixture resembles the leading of traditional stained glass.

Mix powdered poster color and white glue to the desired consistency (thick enough to have body but thin enough to pass through the tip of a squeeze bottle) and place in a plastic container with a narrow tip. Hold a drawing underneath a sheet of acetate or Mylar, and squeeze out the glue mixture to follow the lines of the drawing. Let the glue mixture dry, then repeat to build up the leading to a thickness of about 1/8 to 1/4 inch.

Mix the catalyst and resin according to the manufacturer's specifications for thin castings, and pour into the prepared mold. If some resin spills over the edges, it can be cleaned away with a needle or knife after the material gels. When the casting is fully cured, peel off the backing sheet and apply cut pieces of tissue paper using a brush and heavily catalyzed resin.

Pour the resin over the glue and poster color mold. If excess resin spills over the edges allow it to gel.

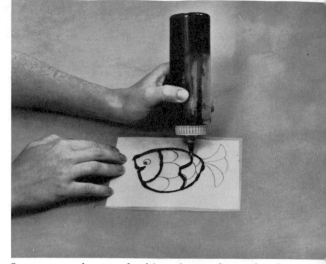

Squeeze a mixture of white glue and powdered poster color onto a sheet of acetate or Mylar, following the lines of a drawing placed underneath.

Mix catalyst into resin in a paper cup marked on the side in ounce gradations. Stir thoroughly until all hairlines disappear.

Trim away gelled resin with a sharp instrument. When the piece is fully cured, peel off the backing and apply tissue paper with freshly mixed catalyzed resin.

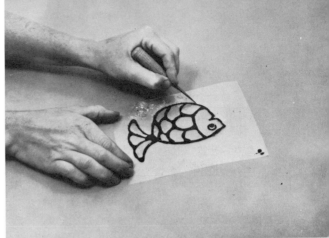

White glue mixed with powdered poster color forms the leading in this large (18-inch) sun medallion.

A window treatment of free-form shapes. Bubbles can be incorporated in the resin and catalyst mixture by stirring vigorously with a paintbrush.

Wire

Wire also makes an attractive substitute for stained glass leading. Copper or aluminum wire is ideal for jewelry-size pieces, while heavier galvanized wire can be used for large medallions.

First, wind the wire around a variety of objects to produce a number of different shapes. Dip the underside of the wire shapes into white glue and lay them on a piece of tissue paper. When dry, trim off the excess tissue and arrange the pieces in a decorative pattern on a sheet of acetate. Secure the pieces with liquid solder (a plastic substance that has the appearance of metal) and attach a metal ring for hanging. Finally, repeat the steps described above for mixing, pouring, and trimming the gelled resin.

An alternative method is to join the metal shapes with liquid solder before adding tissue paper. The resin is then poured and allowed to harden, the backing sheet removed, and cut pieces of tissue paper applied with freshly catalyzed resin.

Assemble the pieces on a sheet of acetate, and join the parts with liquid solder.

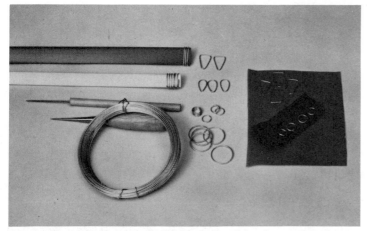

Wrap wire around assorted objects to produce interesting shapes. Dip the wire shapes in white glue, and place on tissue paper. When dry, trim away the excess paper.

Jewelry size medallions shimmer in the light.

Heavy galvanized wire outlines each segment of this large medallion. The plastic was poured and gelled resin trimmed away before tissue paper was applied to the underside.

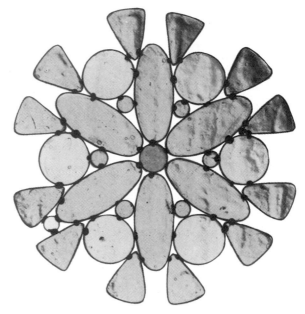

Clay

In this method clay is used to make a mold for resin and tissue paper is brushed on the hardened casting. Leading, squeezed from a tube of liquid metal, is applied as a final step.

Roll out the clay to an even thickness on a sheet of acetate. Cut an opening of any desired shape, pour in catalyzed resin, and let harden. Geometrical shapes are illustrated, but other designs such as flowers or fruit are also effective.

Place the cured casting over a drawing of the desired design and apply tissue paper with over-catalyzed resin. Allow to harden, then apply leading lines from a tube of liquid metal. Use the liquid metal to attach a wire loop at the top, and the medallion will be ready for hanging.

The hardened resin will separate easily from both clay and acetate backing.

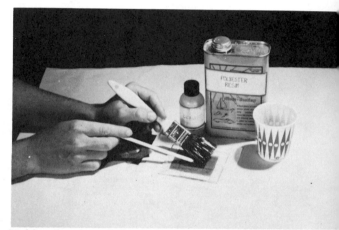

Hold a drawing of the desired pattern under the plastic and apply cut tissue paper shapes with highly catalyzed resin.

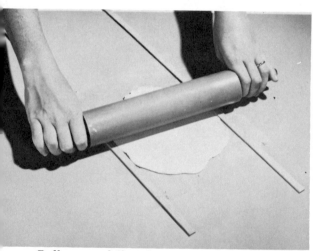

Roll out modeling clay to an even thickness on a sheet of Mylar or acetate.

Cut out segments of the clay by tracing around a pattern or by drawing freehand. Pour catalyzed resin into the molds and allow to cure.

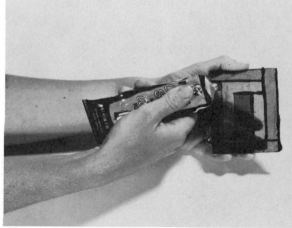

When the resin is completely cured, squeeze on leading from a tube of liquid metal.

The completed medallions.

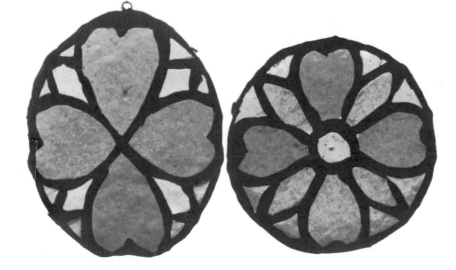

14

MISCELLANEOUS TECHNIQUES

Braid

Objects that are both decorative and useful can be made by braiding tissue paper and wrapping the strands around a mold. Ample glue is used wherever the paper joins so that when the mold is removed the braided shape is rigid enough to stand by itself.

Begin by cutting tissue paper lengthwise into quarters. A thicker braid can be made by using wider strips, a finer braid by dividing the paper into smaller sections. Crush each strip slightly, trying, if possible, to bring the edges in toward the center so

that they will not be visible in the finished plait.

Fasten the ends securely to a tabletop or other firm surface and begin to braid. When you reach the end of one strand, fasten on a second with white glue and conceal the joint in the next plait. To avoid tangled ends, it helps to stagger the lengths of the strands, so that there will always be one long, one medium, and one short length to work with. Continue braiding and adding strands until the desired length is reached.

A mold can be made from any object that has no undercuts and can be removed

230

Wastebaskets from multicolor braided tissue paper. The smaller wastebasket has handles for carrying. Both are waterproofed inside with a coating of thinned white glue and protected on the outside with a spraying of clear mat-finish acrylic.

Cover the mold with plastic wrap and wind with braid, glueing as you go. Newspaper is used here to "fatten" a mold of kitchen canisters to the desired width.

Cut tissue paper lengthwise and crush lightly, bringing the sides to the center.

Clip the ends together to hold them secure and braid the crushed strips. Use white glue to fasten on extra strips to lengthen the plait.

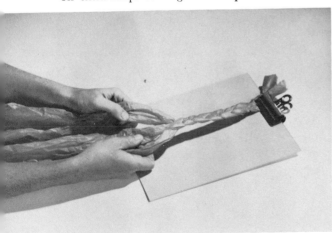

Taper the ends of the braid for an inconspicuous finish. To make a circular top, wind braid on a flat surface covered with plastic wrap. For the two parts to fit together perfectly, wind the top clockwise and the base counterclockwise, then glue together where the ends meet.

Spray the braided shape with mat-finish clear acrylic to protect the surface from dirt and moisture.

easily once the braid is fully wound. Coffee canisters, wastebaskets, flowerpots, and kitchen mixing bowls are all suitable. Wrap the mold with kitchen plastic wrap to prevent it from sticking to the tissue paper, then begin winding the braid. Where each coil meets the next, apply a generous amount of white glue from a plastic squeeze bottle. The glue not only holds the parts, it also gives considerable strength to the finished object.

When nearing the end, undo the braid partway and trim a little from each strand so that when rebraided the strands will taper to a narrow end rather than finishing in an unsightly bulge.

Allow the glue to dry completely, then remove the mold. The plastic wrap will adhere to the tissue paper but can be pulled away easily.

Canister covers. Loops are used to lift off the braided covers, which conceal canisters of tea and coffee.

If desired, the inside surface of a braided object can be waterproofed by brushing on a coating of white glue thinned with water. The exterior can be treated in the same manner, but since the glue mixture dries to a shiny finish, it may be preferable to protect the outer surface from dirt and moisture by spraying with a coat of mat-finish spray acrylic.

Twisted Cord

Twisted cord made from tissue paper can be wrapped around bottles or glasses for a raffialike finish, pressed onto a cardboard backing for coasters, place mats, or hot pads, wrapped around Easter eggs, or even used for macramé or crochet. The cords are not only colorful; because they are twisted so many times they are also remarkably strong.

Cut tissue paper strips in uniform widths of one to four inches. The strips can be twisted by hand, but it is easier to do it mechanically. One choice is to use a hand drill, securing the loose end to a tabletop and inserting the other end in the drill bit opening. Another alternative is to knot the tissue paper around one beater of an electric mixer (remove the other beater) and turn the mixer on to a slow speed. Either method produces cords of uniform thickness. Additional lengths can be added before or after twisting.

Completed objects should be protected from dirt and moisture by coating with thinned white glue, lacquer, or shellac, or, if a glossy surface is undesirable, they can be sprayed with mat-finish acrylic from an aerosol can.

A macramé design in twisted paper cord.

Strips of tissue paper can be twisted mechanically using a hand drill, as shown, or an electric mixer with one beater removed.

Colorful strands of tissue paper cord decorate an Easter egg.

Laminated Paper

Tissue paper assumes a new appearance when a number of layers are laminated together. It loses its transparency and becomes an opaque material that is malleable when damp but dries to a porcelainlike hardness. Decorations made from laminated paper are especially attractive when made into blossoms for flower arrangements or to decorate wreaths or candle holders. They can also be cut and shaped into colorful holiday ornaments that will last for many seasons.

Start by cutting a number of sheets of tissue paper to uniform size. Lay the first sheet on a piece of kitchen plastic wrap and coat the bottom half with thinned

white glue. Fold the top half over the glue-spread area, cover with plastic wrap, and go over the surface firmly with a rubber roller. Remove the plastic wrap and continue adding tissue paper until between six and ten layers are built up.

Allow the laminated paper to dry until damp but no longer wet. To prevent drying beyond this point, wrap securely in aluminum foil. The paper can be kept this way for several days without drying out.

While damp, the laminated paper can be cut and shaped in a number of ways. It can be fashioned into flower petals, scalloped and rolled into paper roses, or wrapped around a dowel or other such object to form spiral decorations. Once dry, a coating of spray lacquer or spray acrylic will bring out. the gloss beautifully.

Place tissue paper on a sheet of clear plastic wrap and brush with thinned white glue.

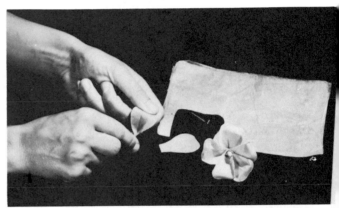

Lay on the second layer of tissue paper and cover with plastic wrap. Press firmly with a rubber roller. Continue adding tissue paper until between six and twelve layers are built up.

While the laminated paper is still damp it can be stretched and molded, and will retain its shape when dry. Here petals are cut and shaped, then fastened together with a brass paper fastener. When dry, add gloss by spraying with lacquer or clear acrylic.

A yellow flower made from laminated tissue paper has a button for its center. Flowers such as these would enliven a Christmas wreath, or would be attractive clustered around the base of a candle.

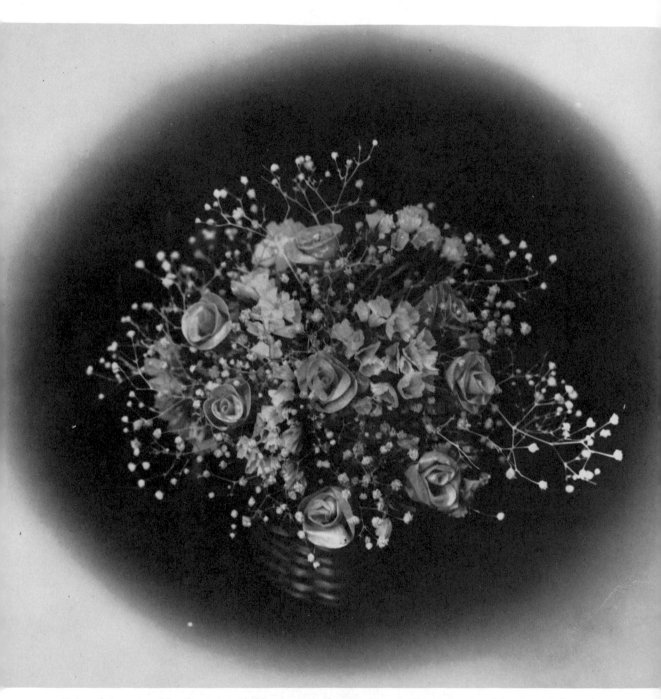

Baby pink roses add color to a miniature arrangement of everlastings. A strip of laminated tissue is cut with a scalloped edge, then rolled up from one end to make each rose.

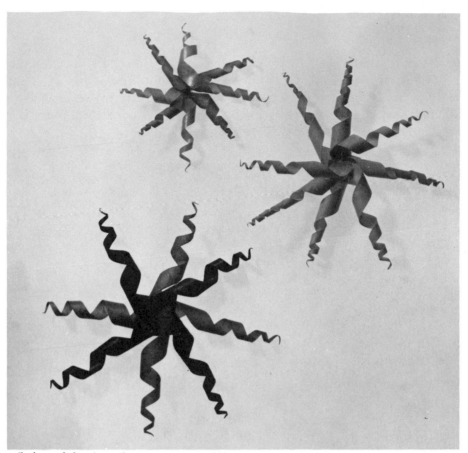

Strips of laminated paper are wound around a wooden dowel, then glued together to make colorful hanging decorations.

Candles

Tissue paper cutouts can be applied to candles in much the same way as to any other surface. The only difference is that the finished design, instead of being coated with lacquer or plastic spray for protection, is dipped into melted wax. As a result the design appears embedded in the candle rather than glued on the surface.

Start with a ready-made candle or make one yourself using supplies and directions available at hobby shops. Glue cut tissue paper designs to the surface using spray cement or white glue. For written messages such as "Happy Birthday" or "Merry Christmas," write the chosen lines on a piece of white tissue paper and glue to the surface of the candle. When the candle is dipped in melted wax, the white tissue paper will become almost invisible and only the writing will stand out.

Melt candle wax in the top of a double boiler or in a coffee can set in a pan of hot water. Make sure that there is enough wax in the container to completely cover the decorated candle. Secure the candle either by tying a length of string to the wick or, in the case of homemade candles, by leaving enough extra wick to hold firmly for dipping. Lower the candle into the melted wax up to the base of the wick, then immediately lift out. If the candle stays too long in the hot wax, the wax under the design will melt and the design will slide off. To avoid streaks and air bubbles move the candle smoothly in and out of the melted wax. Once it has been lifted from the wax, set the candle on a level surface so that the base of the candle will harden smooth and flat.

Designs on egg-shaped candles are cut from tissue paper and glued on with spray cement. The candle is then dipped briefly in melted wax so that the design appears embedded.

A birthday candle with clowns cut from tissue paper. The lettering, the balloon strings, and the clown faces are all drawn on white tissue paper that becomes nearly invisible when the candle is dipped in melted wax.

SELECTED
BIBLIOGRAPHY

ASH, BERYL, and DYSON, ANTHONY. *Introducing Dyeing and Printing*. New York: Watson-Guptill, 1970.

BARRETT, CYRIL. *Op Art*. New York: Viking Press, 1970.

BINYON, HELEN. *Puppetry Today*. New York: Watson-Guptill, 1966.

BLACKHAM, OLIVE. *Shadow Puppets*. New York: Harper, 1962.

BOTHWELL, DORR, and FREY, MARLYS. *Notan: The Dark-Light Principle of Design*. New York: Reinhold Book Corp., 1968.

BRIGADIER, ANNE. *Collage: A Complete Guide for Artists*. New York: Watson-Guptill, 1970.

CUNDY, H. MARTYN, and ROLLETT, A. P. *Mathematical Models*. 2nd ed. Oxford: Oxford University Press, 1961.

HAWLEY, WILLIS MEEKER. *Chinese Folk Design: A Collection of Cut Paper Designs Used for Embroidery*. New York: Dover Publications, 1971.

HELBRONNER, R. *Helbronner's Manual of Paper Flower Making*. London: Berlin Repository, 1858.

HOLLANDER, ANNETTE. *Decorative Papers and Fabrics*. New York: Van Nostrand Reinhold, 1971.

HONDA, ISAO. *Mon-Kiri Playtime*. Tokyo: Japan Publications Trading Co., 1967.

———. *Monsho: Family Crests for Symbolic Design*. Tokyo: Japan Publications Trading Co., 1963.

———. *The World of Origami*. Tokyo: Japan Publications Trading Co., 1965.

HUNTER, DARD. *Papermaking: The History and Technique of an Ancient Craft*. 2nd ed. New York: Alfred A. Knopf, 1947.

JOHNSON, PAULINE. *Creating with Paper*. Seattle: University of Washington Press, 1958.

KASAHARA, KUNIHIKO. *Creative Origami*. Tokyo: Japan Publications Trading Co., 1967.

LALIBERTÉ, NORMAN, and MOGELON, ALEX. *Silhouettes, Shadows and Cutouts*. New York: Reinhold Book Corp., 1968.

NEWMAN, THELMA R. *Plastics as an Art Form*. Rev. cd. Philadelphia: Chilton Book Co., 1969.

RANDLETT, SAMUEL. *The Best of Origami*. New York: Dutton, 1963.

REINIGER, LOTTE. *Shadow Theaters and Shadow Films*. New York: Watson-Guptill, 1970.

RÖTTGER, ERNST. *Creative Paper Craft*. New York: Reinhold Book Corp., 1961.

SCHÖNEWOLF, HERTA. *The Art and Techniques of Shadow Theater*. New York: Reinhold Book Corp., 1968.

STEIN, SIR MARC AUREL. *Serindia*. 5 vols. Oxford: Clarendon Press, 1921.

WENNINGER, MAGNUS J. *Polyhedron Models*. Cambridge: Cambridge University Press, 1970.

———. *Polyhedron Models for the Classroom*. Washington, D.C.: National Council of Teachers of Mathematics, 1966.

WOODY, RUSSELL O. *Painting with Synthetic Media*. New York: Reinhold Publishing Corp., 1965.

YAMADA, SADAMI, and ITO, KIYOTADA. *New Dimensions in Paper Craft*. Tokyo: Japan Publications Trading Co., 1966.

GLOSSARY

Acetate. Cellulose acetate, a thin plastic, is available in rolls and sheets in a variety of weights. It can be used for making puppets, for stiffening lampshades, or as a backing sheet for casts of polyester resin.

Acetone. A strong solvent that can be used to clean dried emulsion glue and catalyzed plastic resin. It is highly flammable and should only be used where ventilation is adequate.

Acrylic Glaze (Liquid Acrylic). A non-yellowing, water-clear varnish with an acrylic resin base that can serve as adhesive as well as glaze. It can be thinned with mineral spirits or turpentine.

Acrylic Paints. A polymer emulsion paint with an acrylic base. Acrylic paints can be thinned with water, but dry to a permanent, waterproof finish.

Adhesive-backed Film. A transparent, vinyl film with a pressure-sensitive adhesive backing that permanently bonds on contact to most dry surfaces.

Aniline Dye. Dyes in a wide range of brilliant colors made from aniline, a derivative of coal tar.

Bristol Board. Smooth white paper of postcard weight or more, with the thickness measured in terms of layers or plies.

Catalyst. A material added to liquid polyester resin to initiate polymerization.

Collage. A composition consisting of elements pasted onto a ground.

Cure. The hardening of liquid plastic resin after the catalyst is added.

Dry Mounting. A method of adhering materials to a flat surface. Heat is used to melt the adhesive coating on dry mounting tissue and to bond the two layers together.

Enamel. A liquid paint consisting of glossy varnishes mixed with pigments.

Epoxy Glue. An adhesive of great strength that is generally activated by mixing two parts.

Foam Core Board. A laminated, lightweight board in several thicknesses that consists of a sandwich of expanded polystyrene foam covered on both sides with white paper.

Gel. An intermediate stage in the polymerization of polyester resin reached when the plastic resembles gelatin. The gelled material can be trimmed or cut with a knife.

Gel Medium. A pure, polymer emulsion in thick, viscous form that can serve as a strong adhesive.

Gesso. A white compound for priming canvas or board to prepare for painting or for collage.

Hardboard. A rigid board in ⅛- and ¼-inch thicknesses made by compressing wood fiber.

Illustration Board. Single or double thickness boards made by mounting drawing paper onto a stiff cardboard backing.

Lacquer. A fast-drying coating in crystal-clear or colors. Because of its strong solvent base, clear lacquer should not be used over spray-painted surfaces, but it will not harm surfaces coated with an emulsion paint.

Laminate. To add layers one on top of the other and bond into a single unit.

Laminating Film. A thin, transparent film used for protecting surfaces from dirt and moisture. Upon the application of heat (either in a dry mounting press or with an iron) the thermoplastic adhesive coating the film melts and bonds the film to the surface below.

Latex Paint. A water-based emulsion often used as house paint. White latex paint can substitute for gesso when priming hardboard or canvas.

Liquid Metal, Liquid Solder. Plastic compounds sold in tubes that have the appearance of metal when hardened.

Mountain Fold. An origami fold in which the sides of the paper are folded down from the crease line to resemble a mountain. Opposite of valley fold.

Mylar. A thin, dense, particularly strong plastic film. When coated with a heat-sensitive adhesive it serves as laminating film. A thicker version, resembling acetate, can be used as a backing for casts of liquid polyester resin; when the resin hardens the Mylar can be pulled away, leaving a smooth surface.

Origami. The art of Japanese paper folding.

Pantograph. A mechanical device used for making enlargements or reductions of a drawing.

Polymer Emulsion. A suspension of plastic resin in water. When the water evaporates resin particles join together to form a clear, waterproof film.

Polymer Medium. Available in both gloss or mat finish, polymer medium can be used as an adhesive, as a varnish, or to thin polymer paints. Milky white when applied, it dries to a clear, waterproof film.

Polymer Paints. Paints with a synthetic resin base. If the resin is an acrylic, they are known as acrylic paints. The paints can be thinned with water, but dry permanent and waterproof.

Polymerization. The process of similar molecules joining into larger molecules. In the case of liquid plastics, polymerization is initiated by the addition of a catalyst, and causes the liquid to become a hard, solid substance.

Rubber Cement. A viscous adhesive made of gum rubber dissolved in benzol. It does not wrinkle tissue paper or cause it to bleed, and is virtually invisible when applied in a thin coat. Since it deteriorates with time, it should not be used for permanent work.

Spray Acrylic (Spray Plastic). A clear acrylic plastic in spray form that can be used to protect surfaces from dirt and moisture. It is available in gloss or mat finish.

Spray Adhesive. An aerosol adhesive similar to rubber cement in that it is invisible when applied and does not wrinkle or discolor tissue paper. It is claimed that it will not deteriorate with age.

Styrofoam (Expanded Polystyrene Foam). A lightweight polystyrene plastic expanded many times its original volume. It can be cut, painted, or glued, but cannot withstand high heat or the strong solvents contained in some paints and adhesives.

Transfer Lettering. Opaque letters printed on a translucent plastic sheet that can be transferred to any dry, smooth surface by rubbing with a pencil, ballpoint pen, or burnishing tool.

Valley Fold. An origami fold in which the paper is folded up from the crease line to resemble a valley. Opposite of mountain fold.

Wheat Paste. An adhesive made by mixing specially prepared wheat flour and water. It can be used alone or mixed with white glue or polymer medium for use with tissue paper collage.

White Glue. An emulsion glue of polyvinyl acetate resin suspended in water. Creamy white when applied, it dries clear and waterproof.

White Glue, "Tacky" Variety. An especially thick white glue with extra holding power.

INDEX OF SUPPLIERS

UNITED STATES

Tissue Paper

(solid colors and madras)

Austen Display, Inc.
133 West 19th Street
New York, N.Y. 10011

Crystal Craft Art Tissue
Crystal Tissue Co.
Middletown, Ohio 45042

Party Bazaar
390 Fifth Avenue
New York, N.Y. 10018

Spectra Art Tissue
Bemiss-Jason Corp.
3250 Ash Street
Palo Alto, California 94306

(white wrapping tissue)

Crystal Tissue Co.
Middletown, Ohio 45042

Acrylic Glaze (Liquid Acrylic)

Protect-It Clear Acrylic Varnish
Connoisseur Studio, Inc.
Louisville, Kentucky 40207

Adhesives

Clear Adhesives

Ambroid Extra Fast Drying Liquid Cement
Ambroid Co.
Weymouth, Massachusetts 02188

Duco Cement
E. I. duPont de Nemours & Co.
Wilmington, Delaware 19898

Rubber Cement

Best-Test Rubber Cement
Union Rubber & Asbestos Co.
P.O. Box 1040
Trenton, New Jersey 08606

Columbia Rubber Cement
Columbia Cement Co., Inc.
150 Ingraham Street
Brooklyn, N.Y. 11237

Spray Adhesives

Krylon Spray Adhesive
Krylon, Inc.
P.O. Box 390
Norristown, Pennsylvania 19404

Scotch Spray Mounting Adhesive
3M Company
Adhesives, Coatings and Sealers
Division
3M Center
St. Paul, Minnesota 55101

White Glue

Elmer's Glue-All
The Borden Chemical Co.
350 Madison Avenue
New York, N.Y. 10017

Sobo Glue
Slomons Labs
Dept. AG68
Long Island City, N.Y. 11101

(extra thick white glue)

Tacky White Glue
Aleene's, Inc.
9119 E. Las Tunas
Temple City, California 91780

Adhesive-backed Plastic Film

(kitchen quality)

Con-Tact Transparent
Comark Plastics Division
United Merchants and Manufacturers,
Inc.
1407 Broadway
New York, N.Y. 10018

(art quality)

Book Laminate
Gaylord Bros., Inc.
P.O. Box 710
Stockton, California 95201

Circle Cutter

Cardbild Circle Cutter
(available from:
Edmund Scientific Co.
300 Edscorp Building
Barrington, New Jersey 08007)

Dry Mounting Tissue (Waxy)

Fotoflat
Seal, Inc.
Roosevelt Drive
Derby, Connecticut 06418

Dyes

(aniline and other dyes)

Aljo Mfg. Co.
116 Prince Street
New York, N.Y. 10012

Fezandie & Sperrle, Inc.
Leeben Color & Chemical Co., Inc.
103 Lafayette Street
New York, N.Y. 10013

(fabric dyes)

Fibrec Dye
Fibrec Dye Center
2795 16th Street
San Francisco, California 94103

Rit
Best Foods Division
Corn Products Co.
Indianapolis, Indiana

Foam Core Board

Fome-Cor
Monsanto Co.
Fome-Cor C3SG
800 N. Lindbergh Boulevard
St. Louis, Missouri 63166

General Art Supplies

Arthur Brown and Bros., Inc.
2 West 46th Street
New York, N.Y. 10036

Flax's
250 Sutter Street
San Francisco, California 94108

A. I. Friedman, Inc.
25 West 45th Street
New York, N.Y. 10036

General Craft Supplies

American Handicrafts
Tandy Corp.
1001 Foch Street
Fort Worth, Texas 76107

Dick Blick
P.O. Box 1267
Galesburg, Illinois 61401

J. C. Larson Co., Inc.
7330 N. Clark Street
Chicago, Illinois 60626

LeeWards
840 N. State Street
Elgin, Illinois 60120

Magnus Craft Materials
109 Lafayette Street
New York, N.Y. 10013

Knives (Mat and Stencil)

Grifhold Knives
Griffin Mfg. Co., Inc.
1656 Ridge Rd. E.
Webster, N.Y. 14580

Stanley Tools
600 Myrtle Street
New Britain, Connecticut 06050

X-Acto Knives
X-Acto, Inc.
48-41 Van Dam Street
Long Island City, N.Y. 11101

Lacquer (Brushing Lacquer)

*Patricia Nimocks Oriental Lacquer
Finish*
Connoisseur Studio, Inc.
Louisville, Kentucky 40207

Laminating Film

Seal-Lamin Laminating Film
Seal, Inc.
Roosevelt Drive
Derby, Connecticut 06418

Liquid Metal

*Duro Liquid Steel, Duro Plastic
Aluminum*
The Woodhill Chemical Corp.
Cleveland, Ohio 44128

*MagiCraft Craft Lead, MagiCraft
Craft Steel*
Magic American Chemical Corp.
Cleveland, Ohio 44128

Liquid Solder

Duro Liquid Solder
The Woodhill Chemical Corp.
Cleveland, Ohio 44128

LePages Liquid Solder
LePages, Inc.
Essex Avenue
Gloucester, Massachusetts 01930

Liquid Watercolors

Ecoline
Talens & Sons, Inc.
P.O. Box 453
Union, New Jersey 07083

Dr. Ph. Martins Liquid Watercolors
(available from:
Arthur Brown and Bros., Inc.
2 West 46th Street
New York, N.Y. 10036)

Medical Applicators

Peerless Applicators
Diamond Match Division
Diamond National Corp.
New York, N.Y. 10017

Oil-base Felt Pen Ink

Flo-Master Inks
Esterbrook
Cherry Hill, New Jersey 08034

Marsh Marking Pen Ink
Marsh Stencil
Belleville, Illinois 62222

Polyester Resin (Liquid Plastic)

The Castolite Co.
Woodstock, Illinois 60098

Natcol Crafts, Inc.
P.O. Box 299
Redlands, California 92373

Polymer Paint, Medium, Gel, Gesso

Hyplar
M. Grumbacher Co.
460 West 34th Street
New York, N.Y. 10001

Liquitex
Permanent Pigments, Inc.
2700 Highland Avenue
Cincinnati, Ohio 45212

Punches

C. S. Osborne & Co.
Harrison, New Jersey 07029

Tandy Leather Co.
Tandy Corp.
1001 Foch Street
Fort Worth, Texas 76107

Scalloping Shears

Wiss Skalloping Shears
J. Wiss & Sons Co.
33-T Littleton Avenue
Newark, New Jersey 07107

Spray Acrylic (Spray Plastic)

Blair Spray Clear
Blair Art Products, Inc.
Memphis, Tennessee 38122

Krylon Crystal Clear
Krylon, Inc.
P.O. Box 390
Norristown, Pennsylvania 19404

Spray Dye

Spray Mark Transparent Color Dyes
Acrolite Aerosol Corp.
84-00 73 Avenue
Glendale, N.Y. 11227

Stencil Punches

Aiko's Art Materials Import
714 N. Wabash Avenue
Chicago, Illinois 60611

Seiwa Kakō Kabushiki Kaisha
3-72 Totsuka-machi
Shinjuku-ku
Tokyo, Japan 160

Transfer Lettering

Instantype, Inc.
7005 Tujunga Avenue
North Hollywood, California 91605

Letraset, Inc.
2379 Charleston Road
Mountain View, California 94040

UNITED KINGDOM

Acetate, Art Papers, Colored Tissue Paper

F. G. Kettle
127 High Holborn
London, W.C.1

Paperchase Products Ltd.
216 Tottenham Court Road
London, W.1

Adhesive-backed Plastic Film

Libra-Seal
William Johnson & Sons, Ltd.
Spindle Way
Crawley, Sussex

General Craft Supplies

Dryad Ltd.
Northgates, Leicester

Polyester Resin (Liquid Plastic)

Alec Tiranti Ltd.
72 Charlotte Street
London, W.1

Polymer Paint, Medium, Etc.

Cryla
George Rowney & Co., Ltd.
P.O. Box 10
Bracknell, Berkshire

Tools

Buck and Ryan
310 Euston Road
London, N.W.1

INDEX